TALES OF A THREE-LEGGED NEWT

Essays and Anecdotes for
Amateur Astronomers

by

Thomas Watson

Tales of a Three-legged Newt
by Thomas Watson
Copyright © 2017 by Thomas Watson
All rights reserved.

ISBN: 197976784X
ISBN-13: 978-1979767842

DESERT STARS PUBLISHING

Other books by this author:

Mr. Olcott's Skies: An Old Book and a Youthful Obsession

Science Fiction

The War of the Second Iteration
Book One, The Luck of Han'anga
Book Two, Founders' Effect
Book Three, The Plight of the Eli'ahtna
Book Four, The Courage to Accept
Book Five, Setha'im Prosh

The Gryphon Stone

Chance Encounters: Three Short Stories

179 Degrees From Now: Short Fiction

This one is for the members of the Cloudy Nights forum and the Tucson Amateur Astronomy Association.

Clear skies to you all!

CONTENTS

ACKNOWLEDGMENTS

With special thanks to Linda for making sure this book is as error free as possible. Would never have guessed I was marrying a copy editor!

.

TALES

‡

THE UPGRADE TO END ALL UPGRADES

When I was fourteen years old I bought a 60mm refractor from J.C. Penney. I was trying to save up money for a larger instrument, but teenage impatience and the lack of opportunities to earn money in my home town resulted in a smaller instrument. Somehow, I didn't feel like I was settling for less. It was a telescope; I was a happy person. Of course, since this was unfortunately a 60mm department-store special, my interest in visual observing was doomed. Everyone knows that these telescopes bring only disappointment. Hobby killers, "they" call them.

Right.

I spent most of my teen years staring at the night sky through that telescope, any clear night I could get away with it. Fortunately, I didn't know any of the killjoys and naysayers back then. I enjoyed the instrument for what it was and what it could do, studied the Moon and double stars, watched Venus wax and wane, and believe me when I say those nights under the stars with that small telescope changed me forever. Am I an exception that "proves" the rule? From the comments I've received from readers of my book *Mr. Olcott's Skies – An Old Book and Youthful Obsession*, I don't believe so.

Much as I enjoyed using that telescope, however, I always wanted something bigger. We all do that, at some point. And more eyepieces. I spent a lot of time gazing at eyepieces in Edmund Scientifics catalogs, though due to a lack of funds I never bought anything from them. So I used that small refractor regularly the way it originally came out of the box, and I filled spiral notebooks with observations based on star charts I copied in the town library. These matters were the most important in the universe to me at that time. I was a nerd before it was fashionable – long before.

Then I grew up.

It was not the best decision I ever made.

Of course, it was not entirely a matter of choice. These things happen. You get older and things change – even if you don't entirely embrace the concept of adulthood. And I never really did, which is why, in the late summer of 2003, the planet Mars was able to convince me that what I most needed at that point in my life was a telescope. A much bigger telescope.

As I recounted in *Mr. Olcott's Skies*, childhood for me was dominated by fascination with the natural world. The lane on which I lived was unpaved; there were woods and a creek within an easy walk. The town was surrounded by farmland.

This was my playground and unofficial classroom. The people who raised me – parents and grandparents, aunts and uncles – encouraged my investigations with books and the "science kits" so popular in the 1960's. Being of an imaginative nature, I soaked it all up without ever once wondering why I would do so, unaware (for a time) that this was at all unusual. Learning the songs of birds and the names of trees, understanding why wildflowers in spring bloom before trees leaf out, learning what to expect (more or less) from the weather by studying clouds and noting the direction of the wind – this was life.

Life took some strange turns after growing up. I lost the dark, rural skies of my youth by moving to Phoenix and, combined with the numerous distractions of life in the big city, this resulted in the refractor being packed away and more or less forgotten. Oh, it decorated a few apartments I lived in, and I never once considered disposing of it, but it was almost never used. The skies over Phoenix were too bright for much more than Moon-watching, and there were all those other things to do. I ran a small business, dabbled in freelance journalism, wrote books that didn't sell, got married, wrote more books and stories (they still didn't sell) and ultimately went back to school to finish a long-delayed degree in plant biology. That's botany with test tubes, in case you're wondering. And that process led me to Tucson, where my wife and I have lived ever since. One night, taking a walk after dinner, she asked me which constellations were over our heads. Answering her question led to a pair of surprises. The first was that, after all those years, I could still recognize the brighter constellations.

The second was that I could see them at all. It

was only then that what I'd heard about the local light pollution rules, put in place for the sake of nearby observatories, became real for me. Evening walks became a bit more hazardous, due to a tendency on my part to look up as we strolled along. I was already standing with one foot on the comeback trail when Mars became newsworthy.

There'd been other near misses, but there'd always been a reason to say "No, not yet." The clear night sky over Chaco Canyon held me spellbound and sleepless for a night, but we went home to Phoenix after that and other such trips and the Old Scope stayed in its box. (It only came out during the hunt for Halley's comet that ultimately led to thirty years – as of now – of marriage.) Shortly after moving to Tucson, while still a student, we drove out to Kitt Peak as part of our early explorations of the region. There were telescopes for sale in the visitor center. I was tempted, but we were living on one paycheck and student loans at the time, so – no, not yet. Even that night of realization, that while the skies over Tucson were not *dark* they might be dark enough, didn't do it.

In August of 2003, that suddenly changed. I was working as a laboratory technician, a job that paid well enough to meet expenses and leave something left over for hobbies. Mars came as close to the Earth as it ever will again in my lifetime, and the news media was making quite a fuss about it. The Flandrau Science Center, at the University of Arizona where I worked, arranged with the local astronomy club to hold a public viewing of the Red Planet. I saw the announcement in the campus newspaper and talked my wife into attending. On a sultry August Saturday night we joined a sizeable crowd on the grassy east mall of the University. The summer rainy season, the so-called Desert

Monsoon, was experiencing a bit of a local downturn, but storms elsewhere were blowing out and sending rafts of debris clouds over the city. We managed quick looks at Mars through a couple of telescopes as it was alternately revealed and obscured by monsoon clouds. What we saw was amazing, but by then Mars had already served its purpose. I was surrounded by telescopes, walking through a field of telescopes.

I was all grown up and it was finally time to buy another telescope. A larger telescope.

That sounds so calm and reasoned. To be honest, I was having a flashback to those younger days, walking around dazzled by the assembled gear and trying not to trip over my own feet. Here around me were instruments beyond anything I'd dreamt of as a boy, and people were quoting prices that were, on current income, possible. My wife probably heard something in me snap. That would have been the connection between the boy I was and the present-day adult contracting like a length of elastic suddenly released. Three decades of strain released in a moment.

One of the advantages of having grown up is that I have just a little more patience than the fourteen-year-old who bought that now venerable refractor. I didn't immediately go to Starizona here in Tucson and hand over my credit card. The Mars viewing events (there ended up being two, and we attended both) made it clear the choice would involve more than deciding between a refractor and a reflector, and simply buying the largest of either that I could afford. I had some research to do.

Fortunately, Al had invented the internet by then.

I gave myself a refresher course on visual astronomy using the old refractor, outfitted now with a couple of Plössl eyepieces and a hybrid diagonal. (I tell this tale in detail in *Mr. Olcott's Skies* I obtained a copy of *Field Book of the Skies* by William Tyler Olcott and used it to pick up where I'd left off all those years ago. And I searched the internet for telescope information and reviews. Searching for reviews led me straight to the Cloudy Nights forum.

That was a game changer.

Having been appalled by some truly vile "discussions" on matters astronomical elsewhere on the internet, I was initially reluctant to do more than lurk at Cloudy Nights. Over the space of about a month, however, I found myself steadily more impressed by and attracted to the civil tone of that forum. I was also, because of the way this virtual place was managed, gleaning far more information from Cloudy Nights than elsewhere. And so, on November 5th, 2003, I logged on for the first time as a member and became a part of that community. The conversations that followed changed the nature of my research. In response to questions I asked, I found myself being asked in turn questions that clarified what exactly I was trying to accomplish. Some of these were matters that might never have occurred to me, until too late. How much money I could spend was an obvious one, and there was already a firm limit in place, but questions regarding interests and possible observing goals took me by surprise. I was even asked how much weight I could safely lift, a question I really should have thought of on my own – but didn't.

Mixed with all of this were a lot of opinionated discussions, light-hearted banter, and personal experience recounted to provide some basis for the many comparisons being made. The cumulative effect was the development of a frame of reference that made it possible for me to base my decision on more than price and aperture alone. My answers painted the picture of a generalist who had as much interest in the Moon, planets, and double stars, as I did in classes of objects I'd never exploited with the small refractor: star clusters, nebulae, and galaxies. When that became clear, specific recommendations began to come my way, the most valuable of which came from hobbyists who thought of themselves as generalists.

This was social media at its most social. While doing my research, I shared observing experiences I enjoyed using the telescope I had, and it was during these discussions of the Moon and double stars in particular, that the 60mm refractor acquired its nickname of Old Scope. As a teenager, visual astronomy had been a solitary affair. Now I was part of a group, interacting with a steadily growing number of people who thought there was nothing at all unusual about me carrying that old refractor up onto the porch roof for a clear view of double stars in Cassiopeia. I didn't have to explain myself or my motives. They got it. They'd all done similar, and sometimes stranger, things for a good look at the night sky.

Autumn turned to winter, and 2003 became 2004. I developed a very clear idea of what I wanted to do with a telescope. I knew what I could spend, and I wanted as much aperture as I could manage in that price range. This led to a series of compromises that ultimately narrowed things down to a single telescope. The first of these involved computerized object location systems. I wanted a significant increase in aperture, but the combination of aperture and computer enhancement ran the price up very quickly. The more bells and whistles the telescope had, the smaller it would be. So – no computers. I opted for an old-school digital system for locating objects. Meaning my fingers, of course. (Aided and abetted by a finder scope.) I wanted tracking, but an equatorial mount with simple drives would cover me there.

With these thoughts in mind, I returned to various catalogs. The year 2004 wasn't very old before I'd settled on the package that seemed just right for me: the Orion SkyView Pro 8EQ. It was late April of 2004, by then. I announced my decision to the Cloudy Nights community and received the usual mixed bag of congratulations, cautions, suggestions for accessories, and ideas for "essential" tweaks to get the most out of the telescope. I couldn't help but be amused by the number of people who shouted "Great choice!" and in the same breath listed all the things about the telescope, focuser, and mount I would need to immediately change before I could get any use out of my investment. I took note of it all, with thanks, and decided I'd change what seemed to need changing as I became accustomed to the instrument.

Okay, I did indulge in some extras due to their frequent – actually insistent would be a more honest word for it – recommendations. I ordered a 2x Barlow lens, and the choice of unit power finder went to the ever popular Telrad. The 25mm and 10mm Plössls that came with the scope, along with the pair of eyepieces I'd obtained earlier for the Old Scope, seemed sufficient for a start. I also picked up a variable polarizing filter for my intended moon-watching. In mid-May of 2004 the budget was ready to take the hit and I placed the order with Starizona. By the end of May, the scope was in the shop and ready to pick up. Dean Koenig had the thing set up so he could instruct me in some basic matters. I was fairly calm about it all, even though the teenager in me, seeing the telescope of his dreams in real life, was going absolutely bananas.

My wife came along with me, that afternoon, and was, I'm afraid, appalled by the massive appearance of the thing. I could see she had reservations, probably regarding storage of the beast. At some point she said something about the ungainly size of the thing, and was taken into the shop to be shown Dobsonian reflectors the size of water heaters. That put things into perspective for her.

I saw nothing over-large or ungainly in the SVP 8EQ. To my eyes it was the picture of stately grace. After so much time with the small refractor, that 8" scope looked pretty impressive. I remember looking at it and thinking, "This will change everything about astronomy for me!"

That was true enough, of course, but I couldn't even begin to imagine the size of that truth.

First Light took care of that.

First Light

Having discussed every other aspect of my upgrade to the SVP 8EQ on Cloudy Nights, it occurred to me that it would be fun to involve them with my First Light experience as well. So I opened a new thread of discussion with the topic, "What Will First Light Be?" The object with the most votes in the end would be the first thing I looked at through my new telescope.

It turned into one of the liveliest and most positive discussions I've ever enjoyed on any online forum. Within a handful of posts a list started to grow. There was no shortage of suggestions, but the Moon, Jupiter, and globular cluster M13 very quickly went to the top and traded places among first, second, and third places more than a few times. Votes were cast and counted. Over the next couple of days the Moon and Jupiter settled in for a race to the top spot, with the M13 hanging tight. As readers of *Mr. Olcott's Skies* already know, these three objects figured prominently in my early development as an observer of celestial sights. The Moon has been a lifelong subject of interest, Jupiter was first light for the Old Scope, and M13 taught me the value of the planisphere. Of course, that book hadn't been written in 2004, so no one participating in that poll could possibly have known this was the case. But I knew, and the symmetry the poll created quite by accident between past and present pleased me no end.

In the end, Jupiter edged out the Moon for First Light object. Symmetry indeed!

The telescope was ready, I was more than ready, and – of course – high thin clouds hazed the skies over southern Arizona for several days after the new telescope came home. Other responsibilities and obligations then intruded when the skies cleared, but finally, on the evening of May 28th, 2004, I found myself setting up the new telescope on a clear Friday evening with a waxing 10-day-old Moon riding high in the eastern sky.

I took it slow, setting up that first night. Though as a teenager I'd often dreamed of owning such an instrument, the experience of setting up and using a 60mm refractor does little to prepare you for balancing an eight-inch reflector on an equatorial mount. I started before sunset to have a bright sky for collimation. The old TV tray I used for an observing table back then bore the instructions that came with the telescope and some annotations made at Starizona. It seemed to take forever to set up, balance, and collimate the scope, but I took the time. I wanted to get it right, and learn the process thoroughly enough that future setups would go more smoothly. Imagine my surprise, when I finished and was ready to go, to discover that it had been a little over thirty minutes.

I knew I needed to wait for the telescope to cool down. May is a nice, warm time of year, here in the Sonoran Desert, but after sundown the air was quickly cooler than the house in which the optical tube assembly had been stored. I understood the concept of tube currents, but thinking the temperature difference wasn't extreme enough to be a problem, I decided to get started. I managed to get Jupiter into the field of view quickly enough, and soon had it locked in with the drives running to keep it centered. Now, here was a boyhood dream come true all by itself: a telescope that held the view steady and left your hands free. Tracking was no longer a desirable concept, it was a happy reality. Then I tried to focus the image.

I focused it again.

"So, that's what tube currents do," I muttered to myself.

A less than desirable concept was also a reality, and one that immediately tested my patience. Jupiter was a quivering blob with smaller blobs arrayed to either side. Ironically, this was a larger scale image of what I remember seeing with the Old Scope, back when neither the scope nor I could be called "old." Then it had been the atmosphere itself to blame, Jupiter being very low in the sky at that time. Now the problem was closer to home. I decided that, having waited this long for a look through the telescope of my dreams, I could wait a bit more, and I made a mental note to investigate the cooling fan options I'd been told about.

While I waited for the scope to come to something resembling equilibrium – it never really did, as quickly as that evening cooled off, though the effect became less pronounced – I learned how easily a Telrad could be aligned. I took care of the optical finder as well. The sky grew ever darker, and overhead small bats swooped around, possibly attracted to the mosquitoes that were being attracted to me.

Night settled in and the mirror cooled down

enough. Back at the eyepiece I was pleased to see that Jupiter hadn't drifted very far from the center of the field of view. It took just a few seconds to realign things. This was First Light for real. The planet was high in the sky and well-positioned for viewing. The sight that greeted me through that relatively low-power (40x) view was a shock to the system. I mean, I *knew* there would be a difference – I was going from 60mm to 203mm in one step – and yet expecting a difference and experiencing it were very different. And that's an understatement if ever I've written one. There was Jupiter, stilling swimming in and out of clarity from time to time, and accompanied by diffraction spikes (which were far more diffuse and less obtrusive than I'd been led to expect), with its dark equatorial belts right where I expected them. The image was not large, but it was bright and had a clarity to it I'd never seen before. The power of aperture and the resolution it provides were immediately evident. Even so, it took a few minutes for my eye-mind connection to truly appreciate what I was seeing; first impressions can be very distracting, but I soon could pick out the more subtle cloud bands.

I stepped back from the eyepiece, an afterimage of the King of Planets fading as I blinked up at the bright "star" most people see when they look at Jupiter in the evening sky. Bright and white, set against a deep blue sky over the twilight world. "This is going to be intense!" I scribbled in my notebook.

I used both eyepieces and the Barlow lens, and settled on the 100x view through the 10mm Plössl. Done messing with equipment for the moment, I simply stood there – yes, I was standing – and tried to take it all in. The Old Scope had never revealed anything of Jupiter except for its prominent north and south equatorial belts. Now I could see just how banded the planet really was, and that the belts and zones had rougher edges than I imagined. Fleeting details, there and gone again, teased me with hints of texture. Since I was not a first-time observer I already knew that patience at the eyepiece is more than a virtue, it's a necessity. My patience was rewarded. Having not truly studied Old Jove, I couldn't put words to what I saw that night, couldn't name what I saw. The Great Red Spot wasn't facing Earth at that time (this was determined after the fact) and the seeing conditions were not perfect (of course not); but none of these things blunted the impact of the sight of Jupiter, its light corralled by an eight-inch mirror and focused by a good eyepiece. The difference between the two Jupiter-oriented First Lights, the one of fond memory and the one I'd just experienced, couldn't have been more profound.

I eventually remembered that I had more than one object to examine on this First Light evening. The Moon was bright and high in the sky, while M13 had yet to clear a tree to the east. Somehow, the great globular cluster had beaten the Moon for second place, in the end, but rather than wait for Hercules to untangle himself from the trees, I turned the reflector up to look at the Moon. I used the 25mm Plössl to start, and in short order the Moon was in the eyepiece and in focus. My old friend from childhood and lifelong companion, the Moon. The sight brought tears to my eye.

Then I remembered the variable polarizing filter.

That was a big improvement. It was easily attached and adjusted, and with it in place I could appreciate and enjoy the view, instead of being dazzled by it. And that view – well...

Unlike Jupiter, the Moon was something I knew

very well, indeed. As a boy I'd become caught up in the great race to the Moon, and our natural satellite was always the favored subject of observation, whatever optical instrument I had. The Moon can impress even in cheap toy telescopes and old binoculars. Small as the Old Scope was, it opened the Moon up to me in my teens. I spent many evenings in my late childhood and early adolescence following the terminator, that ragged and complicated division between night and day on the Moon, learning the names of mountain ranges and craters. In the months between the close encounter with Mars and the night of First Light, I'd spent a lot of time re-acquainting myself with the Moon, relearning the names of things to be seen on the side of it forever turned toward Earth. I knew the place well, or thought I did.

It was the aperture and resolving power effect again. It's difficult now, many years after that night, to really recapture and relate the effect of seeing the Moon with so much more aperture at my disposal. I knew those craters and mountains, and yet – I didn't. Features and details barely visible through the smaller telescope stood out in sharp relief. Central peaks in craters weren't just bright spots that cast ink-black shadows; they were mountains with distinct shapes, seen as if from a high altitude. This is, in a sense, the truth of it. Using combinations of Plössls and the Barlow lens, I flew closer to the Moon that night in my imagination than had ever before been possible. I traveled the terminator, marveling at the complexity revealed in the face of the Moon. It was the next best thing to being there.

I realized then and there I was going to need more detailed and up-to-date lunar references.

But I knew enough, that night, to understand in

glorious detail how much of a difference this telescope would make, viewing the Moon. The walled plain Plato was well clear of the terminator, and since I'm especially fond of that region of the Moon, I lingered there for a long while. The mountains of the region - the Montes Alpes, Teneriffe, Caucasus, Apenninus, and Mons Pico - were almost surreal in their detail. The Teneriffes in particular took my breath away. There was a texture and roughness to them I hadn't seen before, and of course could not have seen through the smaller Old Scope, with its more limited resolving power. And then there was Copernicus. I could clearly see terraces inside the walls of that crater, a detail hinted at on good nights with the refractor. I could also see the smaller pits and small craters left when debris splashed back down from the impact that made Copernicus.

The money, time, and trouble had been worth it, just to see the Moon this way. I could write an entire book about looking at the Moon with an eight-inch mirror. Someday, I just might.

When discussing on the CN forum the choices and compromises that came together in the decision to buy an SVP 8EQ, cautions and objections were voiced. I was warned of the extra work that would be required to set up an equatorial mount. I was told the focuser that was then standard would be difficult to use to achieve fine focus, and I was told that the mount was barely up to the weight of the optical tube assembly and would be shaky. That first night I didn't find myself troubled by any of these. Maybe it was just the excitement of the First Light experience, and maybe I just hadn't turned enough focusers or aimed enough equatorial mounts to know. Given that this was a first for me, an argument could be made, I suppose. The focus seemed sharp enough and easily achieved, and whatever vibration was created by using the focuser settled down in two or three seconds, which was fast enough for me. The thought occurred that some people are just too fussy; I still think there's some truth to that, even though I have committed a few upgrades (such as a motorized focuser) in the years since. But I wasn't analyzing the equipment, that first flight over the Moon.

I wasn't done. My feet were getting sore from the standing, and there was one object yet to observe. By now, Hercules was well above the trees, and M13 was available for my viewing pleasure; I intended to take a look no matter how bright the Moonlight.

Swinging the tube around to point to the northeast took a couple of tries, and I needed to loosen the rings and rotate the tube to put the focuser in the right position. I could see that this aspect of an equatorial mount would take some practice, and maybe a third ring around the tube to keep things from sliding out of hand. But this step in the learning curve was quickly behind me, even if for a moment it felt something like walking upstairs backwards, or learning to count back change at a cash register. I used the Telrad to point the scope where I knew the cluster to be, verified with the optical finder that I had the cluster in sight, and locked everything down for tracking. And there was M13, almost dead center in that 25mm Plössl.

I remember thinking that if this was what it looked like with that much Moonlight in the sky, the view might be overwhelming on a darker night. I eventually remembered to breathe regularly, and to play with eyepiece combinations to see what view I liked best. For a while, I didn't feel the need for anything but the 25mm Plössl, and after some experimentation, I ended up using that and the Barlow. Here was an object I hadn't viewed at all, since restoring the Old Scope, even though it was the very first deep-sky object I ever deliberately tracked down, on a warm summer evening many years before. That memory came back to me and I glanced at the head of Draco for a moment with a laugh. It seems so absurd, now, that I could have confused that with the Keystone – but I did, once upon a time.

The cluster was a patch of pale white light that trailed off in ragged edges into the darkness of the universe. There was a grainy look to it, as if a pinch of powdered sugar had been carefully deposited on a bit of black velvet. Or maybe not sugar after all, for as obvious first impressions of its appearance settled into my mind's eye, the glint of stars within the cluster made itself known. None were resolved completely or consistently, flickering on and off as my eye moved and light from different portions of the cluster was swept up by averted vision. The star cluster glittered with ephemeral cold pinpricks of light.

Memory came to the surface, of the night I'd first seen this object in the Old Scope. Dew-soaked sneakers, mosquitoes and fireflies, and the revelation that a planisphere was the key to learning my way around. It had been quite the night. The round, fuzzy patch of light the refractor had revealed was a high point in my young observer's life.

Memory retreated. This experience was off the chart by comparison. Unfair the comparison might be, but it was once again impossible to avoid the stunning sense of contrast.

I could have stared at it forever, but there was one thing I still wanted to look at, another old favorite from younger days. I was beginning to feel the effects, in legs and spine, of standing and staring through an eyepiece for such a long time. But I had to do this. Zeta Ursa Majoris was the first double star I'd ever observed with the Old Scope, and after Mars, the first thing I observed with the Old Scope in 2003. One more time that night I put the Telrad to use, and in a few moments was looking at an old friend. There was Zeta Ursa Majoris and 80 Ursa Majoris, Mizar and Alcor, and near Mizar – though comfortably separated – was the secondary star. Brighter and clearer, more obviously separated, but here at last was a sight for which the Old Scope was not rendered insignificant. It made me realize that, as grand a thing as eight inches of aperture surely was, there would be nights out there, still, with that Old Scope.

I was an altogether happy man, that night. All the research and compromise had come together in an instrument I was sure would serve me well. I had a lot to learn, and even more to see. At my desk, writing up the observing log for First Light, I realized I was more than a little footsore. And my back was seriously stiff. I did indeed want to get out there again very soon, but first I would need to see to an observing chair. And good red light would be useful, as would an eyepiece with a wider field of view. And there was the matter of a lunar map, and...

Well, you all know how that goes.

THE NAME'S THE THING

I didn't call it the SVP 8EQ for very long, and once again I have the Cloudy Nights forum to thank for that.

No, really, I'm grateful.

I've never been much for naming inanimate objects. There's nothing in the slightest bit wrong with the idea, and I've never made fun of people for doing so. At least, not since I discovered that she who was to become my wife had a name for her Honda Civic. But a lot of people do this, and among their ranks are no few amateur astronomers. Among these, at the time that I bought the SVP 8EQ, was a fellow club member with a large Dobsonian reflector named Violet. And for good reason. He'd built this scope and used material for much of it that was the most amazing shade of purple. (The first look I ever had of Omega Centauri was through Violet – not an experience I'm likely ever to forget.) Telescopes with names appear regularly in the signature lines of Cloudy Nights members.

My early involvement with that online community was primarily as a lunar observer in the

Lunar Observing section. There hadn't been much going on in there, and after I'd posted a few times, a fellow Moon-watcher suggested we have conversations there and regularly share observing reports to see if we could enliven things just a bit. Over time, it worked, and more lunar observing enthusiasts began to share experiences and pictures there. It was a grand time, even if it did lead to my becoming a moderator of the "Lunie Bin" as we came to call it – the misspelling being deliberate. When relating observing experiences with the old 6omm, I frequently made reference to its age, which was over three decades by that point. It was my old telescope, source of fond memories, a treasured link to younger days and simpler times. Fellow "Lunies" gradually took to referring to it as that old scope of desertstars' (my CN handle). One of them, one day, capitalized it as Old Scope. I rather liked that, for some reason, and began to use it when writing observing reports. After all, having survived in usable condition for such a very long time, it seemed to deserve that much respect at least.

For a few weeks or so following First Light, the new telescope was simply referred to as "the eight-inch," or "the eight-inch Newt," short for Newtonian. Fair enough; everyone knew which telescope was meant.

The Off Topic Observatory on Cloudy Nights – that portion of the forum set aside for idle chit-chat – changed that. Now, to call this an eclectic group would be a wee bit of an understatement. Usually, this is a good thing, since it means if you're puzzled by something – astronomical or not – you can post about it in that off-topic area and there's a good chance someone has been there and done that. Sometimes such a diverse collection of personalities and opinions can be the stuff of moderator nightmares. In between is a lot of good-natured verbal horseplay. A few weeks after I started using my "Newt" and reporting on my progress, there was an off -topic thread in which a jest was made in the style of Monty Python's Flying Circus. Being a big fan of Pythonesque comedy, I naturally joined in, and at one point someone used the iconic phrase from *Monty Python and the Holy Grail*, "She turned me into a newt!" (I don't remember why.)

I allowed as how newts weren't such a bad thing. After all, I was enjoying the view through mine.

An important distinction was then drawn, that of being turned into a newt, as opposed to being turned *on* to a newt. I'd been turned on to a newt with three legs, and couldn't complain, since things had surely gotten better.

The quality of humor is surely at times strained. And if it droppeth like rain as mercy is said to do, it's sometimes a bit of an acid rain. In this case it was a gentle drizzle, didn't sting, and certainly didn't dampen anyone's enthusiasm. I began to refer to the views through my Three-legged Newt, and the name stuck. Okay, mostly because I kept using it.

A truly minor matter, to be briefly reported with a smirk. It's good to be reminded, from time to time, that we're supposed to be enjoying all of this.

ON A DARK AND WINDY NIGHT

Someone said there would be a gap in the clouds. They'd seen it in satellite images. Not long after sunset was the best guess. I pulled my hat down tighter and turned my jacket collar up against the wind. Optimism was *not* the feeling of the moment.

It was not a promising start for my first time under dark skies with the Three-legged Newt. It sat near the back end of the rented Subaru Outback, shaking as a cool desert wind battered it. The light was fading rapidly, but I could still see dust and grit swirling around the tripod legs. The tube and focuser caps remained firmly in place, and a snug elastic shower cap protected the still pristine primary mirror of the Newt from airborne crud. It was a pink shower cap; I didn't care, so long as it held on tenaciously to the butt end of the telescope. Clouds filled the sky, long rows of tattered dark grey that streamed overhead, shrouding what should have been a deep blue twilight sky.

Word was, there would be a gap, that the clouds were not in fact endless. People kept repeating that, as darkness fell.

I found myself wondering what I was doing, still sitting there after a day of warm, windy overcast. What was it I hoped to accomplish, a triumph of optimism over reality? The idea was to have the Newt under dark skies for the first time. That was the goal. But it seemed the preparations and the drive to this bare, dusty field in the desert had been wasted. Why didn't I just leave and go home?

Because someone said there would be a gap in the clouds.

Regular observing with the Newt had become sporadic when the summer thunderstorm season arrived, and came to a complete stop at the peak of the so-called desert monsoon. As the storms died down and the clouds faded with the memory of another long desert summer, I started making plans to get out of town and see how the Three-legged Newt performed under dark skies. I'd already joined the local astronomy club (Tucson Amateur Astronomy Association) and was looking forward to one of their monthly observing sessions west of the city. But before the weather cooperated in a way that facilitated one of these gatherings, another event came up on the calendar. My first trip to a dark-sky site ended up being The All-Arizona Star Party.

At that time, autumn of 2004, there were two star parties held each year a few miles south of Arizona City, a town that was itself just south of Casa Grande, AZ. There was the All-Arizona Messier Marathon in the spring, and the All-Arizona Star Party in the autumn, meant to celebrate the end of the summer rainy season and the return of clear skies. I learned of the event from members of the local astronomy club, and when it came up for conversation on Cloudy Nights as well, was delighted to learn that several forum members from the Phoenix metro area intended to be there. I'd already decided to go, but the chance to meet a few virtual friends in real life certainly increased my level of motivation.

On Saturday, October 16th, 2004, I loaded the astronomy kit I had then into the Outback and first headed north up the highway to Casa Grande, then doubled back south past Arizona City, along back roads and through a combination of mesquite-dominated desert scrub and soon-to-be-harvested cotton fields. I was flying by the seat of my pants, having never been there before; the map I took from a website didn't inspire confidence. But someone put signs up along the way, and so I found the place on the first try. It took all of 90 minutes to get to the wide, dusty field used for assembling astronomers from Arizona and beyond. At some point the pavement ended and dirt with patches of washboard took the place of the paved road. The Outback's suspension proved more than equal to the challenge, and there were no collimation woes at all when I set the scope up later that evening.

I'm a lover of desert landscapes, and the one I drove through was pleasant enough, with Joseph Wood Krutch's "curious little heaps of mountain" all around me. Not quite a postcard landscape, though, being so heavily overgrazed where it hadn't been converted to farmland. The wind increased as I drove, and the dust devils around me did credible impersonations of F-1 tornadoes. That gave me pause. I'd been warned the Three-legged Newt would be a heavy beast, and there's certainly some truth to this, but I started to wonder, watching those desert twisters, if it would be heavy enough! (No joke – several years later, in the same location, one of these monster dust devils tore up the observing field, upending and seriously damaging a large telescope. I wouldn't have thought it was possible.)

The host club that year was a group from the Phoenix area, and was responsible for the signs along the first part of the drive out into the desert, marking the correct turns. Along one interminable stretch of dirt road, the miles rolled away into the cloud of dust rising behind me, with no signs along the way. I worried that I'd missed a turn and was becoming a bit anxious when, at last, one final sign appeared. The left turn there took me past a small cotton field, and into the observing area. I saw a collection of cars, RVs, and SUVs scattered singly and in small groups all across the area. I found an SUV that matched the description one CN member had given me so I'd be able to spot his camp. Near it was an 18-inch Dobsonian, which I'd also been told to look for. I parked nearby, got out, and took a better look around. There may have been all of twenty vehicles visible, but no signs of life.

Those stalwarts still in attendance were asleep or (as I later learned) in town for lunch. It was definitely a star party though, with a variety of telescopes – wrapped and covered to protect them from dust – standing as if on watch around the cars, trucks, and tents. Dust swirled around with every gust and the scraggly creosote bushes surrounding the site were never still. I got back into the car, slid the seat back, put in the earphones, and relaxed to some Beethoven cello sonatas while waiting. As the warm afternoon passed and the clouds thickened, people began to return from town or emerge from tents and vehicles. Among those coming back, I found some of the Cloudy Nights members I'd hoped to see there. A few of these CN members had been involved in the selection of that First Light list. Familiar faces from TAAA meetings appeared, as well. Many of these departed as the evening came on, headed for home, since the weather was growing cloudier, not clearer, and some of them had had quite enough of cloudy skies the night before.

Near sunset, long rifts appeared in the clouds, revealing a lovely two-day-old Moon. Still clinging to a shred of hope, I'd already set up the Newt, and I aimed it at that young Moon. It was a beautiful sight through the telescope, a delicate curve of light that seemed rather fanciful with the veils of cloud streaming over it. I'd been joking all along that if I saw anything at all through the scope at this dark (but cloudy) site, I'd call the trip worthwhile. As other observers took turns at the eyepiece to see how the Newt performed, I crossed my fingers that this jest would not come back to haunt me. The rifts closed and the Moon was gone, but the sun lit the clouds from below for a while, and those who remained were treated to a glorious Arizona sunset. Then the wind blasted across the desert with more enthusiasm; a few more people bailed out, and the rest sought shelter.

About an hour after sunset I stepped out of the car, bound for the porta-jon, and wondered as I trudged across the dusty ground if the wind was dying down. Stepping back outside afterward there was no doubt the wind had gentled considerably, and stars were peeking through the flying clouds. Around me, those who had clung to the hope of a gap in the cloud cover were turning on red lights and fiddling with telescopes. The dark clouds overhead were tattered and torn, with the rifts full of stars. North and southeast, where the cities lit the sky, the clouds were a soft grey. The wind died to a whisper and the skies gradually began to clear, first in the southwest, then overhead. The clouds cleared away almost completely for more than two hours, and the Three-legged Newt was under dark skies for the first time.

I'd actually come out there with a plan to observe objects out of my reach from my Tucson back yard. Yes, those are better skies than you find in most cities of any size, but they weren't truly *dark* skies, after all. I was of a mind to seek out galaxies and the Veil Nebula. But all signs pointed to this patch of clear sky being a passing thing, so to save time I changed gears and went after objects that I already knew how to find. Even as I tracked down objects in the sky, the wind started to make a comeback, quiet one moment, assertive in the next. I made what time I had count. I had excellent views of M22, M11, M8, M24, and M57. It was almost disconcerting to see the Ring Nebula with so many stars in the field of view. I found Neptune for the first time. And, of course, I spent some time just standing there and looking up at the star-filled sky and the westering Milky Way.

I managed to remember that this was a gathering of like minds, and that fellow enthusiasts with telescopes larger than mine were set up in the darkness around me. A fellow TAAA member with a large Dobsonian was not far away, so I left the Newt for a while to see what he was up to, and was given a look at the planetary nebula NGC 40 and a galaxy near beta Andromedae (NGC 404) – Mirach's Ghost. A fellow CN member, using a clone of the Three-legged Newt, offered to share a view of the Helix Nebula (NGC 7293) using an eyepiece with an impressively wide field of view and an appropriate filter. (I've forgotten, now, which one he employed.) The ghostly and graceful sight in that eyepiece put filters and better eyepieces at the top of the list of items to investigate and eventually purchase.

Back at my own telescope, I gave the Helix Nebula a try; the unfiltered view through a 25mm Plössl was disappointing. Then I took aim at beta Andromedae, and was pleased by how easily NGC 404 could be seen.

By then the clouds were coming back, and once again the sky was reduced to patches of stars between starless darkness. The wind rose back to its former strength and persistence. I battened down the hatches and crawled into the Outback to get some sleep. Sleep didn't come easily, between the wind and the coyotes singing. Whenever I woke up, I peered out to see if the skies had opened up again. A couple of hours before sunrise I found myself looking out at stars. Climbing out of the car, I realized there wasn't more than a faint breeze moving the fresh, cool morning air. Saturn was high in the sky. The sky wasn't, sad to say, completely cleared. Venus flirted with pale bars of clouds that reflected light from Tucson. Orion wore a nebulous shroud and more clouds were drifting in. I chose an easy target, and settled in for a long look at Saturn, playing a sort of patience game with gaps in the clouds, but in the end having my best views of Saturn ever. The rings in all their glory, the sharp black thread of the Cassini Division, even the quietly shaded bands of clouds on the planet itself. And Titan. Mustn't forget Titan, of course.

A grey overcast soon covered the sky, growing paler as the dawn approached. It was a quiet sunrise, with the sun itself concealed by clouds. In time, the die-hards straggled out and a few camp stoves were lit; the aroma of coffee drifted through chilly morning air.

That first taste of astronomy away from city lights was certainly sweet, and I resolved that morning, as I packed up and headed into Arizona

City for breakfast, to repeat the experience at the first opportunity. I'd heard it and read it in many posts on Cloudy Nights, that dark skies were like an increase in aperture. Now I knew the truth of it firsthand.

If aperture rules, its kingdom is the dark sky.

THE CHAIR

Very early on I realized that my initial astronomical purchase was not to be my last. To be perfectly honest, I expected as much going in. A lot of accessories were suggested as I went through my public, online selection process, almost all of them prefaced with the phrases "You're going to want" or "You're going to need," as if these matters were a given. I actually made lists of them all, just to keep it straight. It will probably come as no surprise that I wanted or needed fewer things than others might have predicted. Being a fairly casual visual observer, the path of the gear head had no real attraction, but there were a few recommendations that I went along with.

The Barlow lens and the Telrad finder were among the first, coming in with the initial purchase. That Telrad may be the single most effective and valuable add-on I've ever picked up. But as I made that initial purchase, I decided to pull my punches and see what actual use of the Three-legged Newt suggested. After the First Light experience, I said something on Cloudy Nights to the effect that a chair was probably going to top the list. I didn't ask for recommendations, just said my feet and back would appreciate some consideration being shown. And the advice began to pour in.

A couple of commercially available options were immediately suggested, and just as quickly countered with examples of folk making do with bar stools, seats for drummers (not cheap, but frequently available used – which may say something about that profession), and various and sundry other household posterior supports. Then the do-it-yourself crowd chimed in with plans and assurance that building something that might suit me would be easy and far less expensive. Except, of course, for the cost of the tools I'd need to buy for a one-off job. The DIY option was quickly passed up, for my part, but not by a fellow Cloudy Nighter.

The discussion of chairs led to a curious situation that ended up with me owning an observing chair made of wood by one of the DIY crowd on Cloudy Nights. The DIY crowd was quite insistent that this was the best way to fill the need, but to be honest, I have no such skills and have always lacked the motivation to acquire them. As the conversation went on, Ron asked questions about focuser height and my weight, which I at first assumed would assist in recommending a brand. Instead, the information was used to build a suitable chair, and by the time I learned this (he started posting illustrated progress reports) the chair was nearly completed. It was pleasing but a bit embarrassing – I didn't really know the guy, except by posts on the forum. That he would take on such a thing on my behalf, based on a virtual acquaintance, surprised me. Apparently, for people who love working with wood, just about any excuse will do.

I went along with it, and when the chair was

done, Ron and his wife used a trip to my part of the state as an excuse to drop by and deliver the chair. I'll admit to having had mixed feelings about the visit, but those evaporated when they arrived and, within minutes of entering the house, began to browse the book shelves. This is a thing I've learned about people over the years: if someone walks into our house and glances at the wall of books that greets them and makes no comment, or (worse) looks puzzled, they're just visitors. If they gravitate toward the books and start checking titles, we're already friends. These two went right to the books.

Good start.

We chatted for a while, and then the chair was hauled out of their vehicle. It was a beautiful thing made of a combination of attractive hardwoods. We set it up in the driveway, adjusted the seat to a comfortable height, and I sat down. The seat was held in place by friction, the same way as the popular Starbound Observing chair, one of the commercial options often recommended. It looked a damned sight better than one made of steel tubes, to be honest, and I was quite pleased with what Ron had put together. I was about to say so when the friction failed and the chair dumped me on my ass in the driveway.

The look of wide-eyed shock and betrayal on Ron's face was priceless, though I must admit my appreciation of that fact wasn't exactly immediate. I was picking gravel out of the palms of my hands and trying not to make things worse by saying the wrong thing, and any number of wrong things were bubbling around in my head at that point.

Ron helped me up and I said something like, "I take it it's not supposed to do that?"

The guess was made that the product he'd used to bring the shine and color out in the wood wasn't dry enough yet, so we laughed the incident off and I repositioned the seat. This time it seemed to hold well enough.

I managed to get the man to accept some money for the wood he'd used, and after a short but pleasant conversation with them, they continued on with their journey. Later that day my wife came home and was full of admiration for this unusual bit of furniture. I set it up in the living room and sat down to illustrate its purpose.

The seat promptly slipped and dropped me on my ass again. Fortunately, I landed on carpeting this time.

"It's the oil in the wood," I assured her, as she caught her breath. Unlike my visitors earlier in the day, she couldn't resist laughing.

It wasn't the oil, and long story short, at the next All-Arizona Star Party I met up with Ron again and he took The Chair away for adjustment. The solution ended up being a long row of hardwood teeth in the space that accommodated the height adjustment for the seat. It worked perfectly, and for a few years The Chair – it started out on Cloudy Nights as "Tom's Chair," then developed an identity of its own – was a fixture at All-Arizona events and at the TAAA then-monthly observing sessions west of town.

In time, problems with my back and the development of sciatica made The Chair difficult to use. It's a heavy thing, being made of hardwood, and bad discs in my back make loading it into my vehicle problematic. The seat – being flat and also of wood – unfortunately aggravates the sciatica; attempts to attach some sort of cushion to it were less than successful. Some of the chair alternatives suggested before Ron built The Chair were reconsidered, and I ended up owning a lighter, cushioned Starbound Observing Chair. But I never got rid of The Chair – and there were offers made. It's a thing of beauty, and as impractical as it became, even my wife is resistant to parting with it.

And a good thing, too. I've learned to tame the sciatica and, through weight loss and exercise, have improved the condition of my back. Using The Chair at home, at least, is re-entering the realm of possibility.

"YOU FABULOUS PEOPLE!"

On both the Cloudy Nights forum and at meetings of the Tucson Amateur Astronomy Association, I encountered a strong interest in performing public outreach. Since my past involvement in astronomy had been as a teenage misfit in a small town, any social aspect of this hobby was a new idea. But accounts I read of people sharing the view, with both adults and children, appealed to me. And, of course, I'd been the recipient of such outreach in August of 2003, at the Mars viewing event that reignited my desire to be an observer. (I didn't think of it as "outreach" at the time, having never before encountered such a thing.)

So the idea of participating in events such as school star parties was in my mind as I set the parameters for the upgrade. In part because of this idea, I went with an equatorial mount with drives. It made sense to let the telescope do the walking while I did the talking. I was quite eager to get into outreach, back then, but when I bought the Three-legged Newt there was an immediate reality check. I needed to learn to use the durned thing before I could go out in public without making a fool of myself. Fortunately, very soon after I bought the Three-legged Newt, the school year, and the outreach season for 2004, came to an end, and I had plenty of time to practice.

At the October TAAA general meeting I found the opportunity I needed to get started. One of the signup sheets was for an elementary school less than a mile from where I live. The event was to be held just before Thanksgiving. The nearby location simplified the logistics for this first-ever attempt at outreach. I signed up.

Of course, a major storm system rolled through town the day before the star party, bringing needed rain to the desert (even as an astronomer, I can't live in a desert and complain about generous clouds), but also making us very nervous about the viability of this event. The storm cleared out in time for Tuesday the 23rd of November to be clear and calm (with very good seeing conditions), even if it was a bit cold and damp. The party was on! I arrived a bit before seven o'clock to find five TAAA members already there and in the process of setting up a mix of refractors and SCTs; my Newtonian reflector was greeted as a most welcome illustration of yet another telescope type. A fellow club member, finished with his own preparations, hustled over to help me haul my gear to a spot on the concrete basketball court where the others were doing various alignment routines. A scattering of happily hyperactive children were already running amok in the dark – their gathering that evening had involved refreshments in the form of pumpkin pie (with whipped cream), cider, and hot chocolate. (I kid you not, they called the event "Pie and the Sky!") The kids, being well and fully fueled, made me think of particles in high-energy physics experiments – without magnetic containment. They'd been given glow-in-the-dark circlets (don't know what else to call them) and were flinging them about in the dark over the field south of us, chasing them and each other around, with great hue and cry, in the dark.

Rings of blue and green light whirled up into the air, into a sky growing steadily darker, even as the Moon increased in brilliance. Under the Moon, chasing those rings of light, sometimes catching and sometimes not, a couple dozen elementary school children running off all that pie and apple cider – it wasn't exactly what I'd pictured, getting ready for the event, but it didn't fail to bring a smile to my face.

If this all sounds unnerving, such pandemonium so close to a lot of expensive astronomy gear, relax. There were also adults out there keeping the craziness well away from us.

These kids didn't leave any of that energy behind when we announced we were ready for them. Being primed for excitement, they were easily excited by what they saw. I put the Newt on the waxing gibbous Moon (about 11 days old) using a 25mm Plössl so they could see the whole thing, using the variable polarizing filter so they'd still be able to see afterwards. The TAAA member who helped me bring stuff out from the truck used his SCT (possibly a 10" - I'm afraid I didn't take note of the aperture) to show high-power close-ups of the region around Tycho and along the terminator. We bounced kids from one scope to the other, a full view showing Tycho and its rays, then a close-up of the crater and its dark collar of frozen lava. We explained what they were seeing as if telling a story; the kids ate it up as greedily as they had the pie.

For all the noise and energy, it went very well,

and everyone was happy. One of my first customers, in climbing the kitchen stepladder I'd brought for those who were height-challenged by virtue of their age, bumped her head on the focuser on the way up. She couldn't see it in the dark, which in hindsight I should have realized was a risk. No harm done, I re-centered the image and we were fine (aside from considerable mortification on the girl's part), and subsequent visitors were more carefully guided up the steps. Another one steadied herself by grabbing the finder scope before I could react, but again, it took about a minute to re-center the image and lock the clutches. After that I hit on the idea of getting their hands on the top bar of the stepladder to steady them as they went up. Those two were the only mishaps.

Getting them lined up with the eyepiece was no real trouble at all, with the Moon shining through it. I watched the bright Moonlight projected through the eyepiece and onto foreheads, cheeks, and noses. The kids could see it, and followed it like a beacon. Still, I provided guidance in order to avoid nose prints on the lens. At the suggestion of someone more familiar with outreach, I employed a trick that involved making a circle around the eyepiece with thumb and forefinger, and saying, "Look into the circle I make with my fingers." Oriented by that – and my hand showed up clearly with the black telescope tube as background – the kids quickly lined up with the eyepiece. Moonlight took them the rest of the way in.

Many of these kids came back for second (and third and fourth...) looks, by which time they were experts at the eyepiece, and I could answer parental questions without much concern for what was going on at the scope. I ended up on a first-name basis with one pair of brothers who were back at my eyepiece at least a dozen times and were hoping that their request for a telescope would be fulfilled on Christmas morning. I'll never know for sure if it happened, but their father had a lot of questions – asked when his kids were out of range – and he actually took notes from the answers we all gave him.

Speaking of questions, man, did I ever answer questions! Very good questions, from adults and children alike. How far away is the Moon? How long would it take to drive there? (Believe it or not, the fellow showing the close-ups had an answer for that one.) What's the Moon made of? Will its light hurt my eyes? How did craters happen? Did any bits of the Moon come here? At times I had to think fast, when the question dealt with a matter that doesn't often enter into my own observations. But I believe that between us, the small group of volunteers I mean, we handled it well.

The other scopes were showing items that would look good even with so much Moonlight. The 'Double-Double' in Lyra was a popular stop. That was seen through a large refractor, and they were shown the sight in stages: naked eye, it's one star; finder scope, two stars; big scope, four stars. This blew many minds, presented in that fashion. The scope beside mine was on Alberio, and most of the kids exclaimed over the "pretty" colors without prompting. And someone else put the Pleiades in their sights with a wide-angle eyepiece that did the cluster justice. The rest of us stayed on that big, beautiful Moon. Funny thing about that - three scopes on the Moon and the kids still couldn't get enough of La Luna.

Midway through the event a very bright meteor plunged down into the west, trailing sparks. I think most of those present saw it, and you'd have thought we set off fireworks from the reaction. Someone wanted to know how we'd arranged that. Regrettably, it wasn't one of the children, and the woman was dead serious.

It was a two-hour whirlwind of happy, excited children and appreciative parents and teachers, that seemed suddenly and too soon ended. It wasn't until all but a scattering of kids and parents had departed that I realized I was chilled to the bone and dew was running down the tube of the OTA — the only time I can remember dew ever being a problem for me in Arizona. As one family prepared to depart, the mother turned to face the group of us and express her gratitude (hardly the only one, by the way) saying that her family had had a fabulous time. One of her kids, the young girl who had earlier collided with my focuser, shouted, "Yes, thanks, you fabulous people!"

And you know, by that point, I was certainly feeling like a fabulous person. From the grins showing in the dark on the faces of my fellow volunteers, I was not alone.

BUMPS IN THE NIGHT

The world at night is a different place, as any amateur astronomer knows. You hear things and sometimes see things out there in the dark that would otherwise not be experienced. In the years I studied the stars in my youth, I encountered geese migrating high in the night, raccoons and opossums, more fireflies and mosquitoes than can possibly be counted, and a stray horse who appeared to be sleep-walking. As soon as I took up the hobby again, I became reacquainted with the quiet oddities of the night. Living in a suburban area, these at times included encounters with curious neighbors, as well as wildlife. I've heard and seen coyotes and skunks, listened to geckos chirp and bark, been overflown by great horned owls, and even witnessed one of those big, winged predators trying – and failing – to take out a stray cat. All of them part of the night life.

Two such incidents that happened after I ended the astronomy hiatus stand out for me, one with the Newt, the other the Old Scope.

When I decided to get into stargazing again, I still had the old 60mm refractor I started with so many years before, and I put it to good use while figuring out what I was going to buy as an upgrade. One evening, as I was studying the Moon, a male voice hailed me from the alley. "Excuse me, sir," and a bright light was in my face. It wasn't as much of a shock as it might have been, since I'd been staring at a bright first quarter Moon at the time. It still startled me, and my first reaction was less than graceful.

"What the hell's with the light?" I demanded.

"I was trying to see what you had there." The light dropped and it bearer identified himself as a police officer.

"It's a telescope," I said, though I was reasonably sure he'd figured it out by then.

"Ah, yes. You haven't seen anyone else out here, have you? Someone with a gun?"

"Just you," I replied. Okay, I didn't really mean to sound like a smartass. It just slipped out that way. "Why? Something going on? Should I be packing things up?" The idea that someone was wandering around armed, in a way that had attracted the attention of the police, was alarming.

"Not sure. Lady across the way said someone was back here pointing a rifle at jets flying overhead."

I looked up as a jet from the nearby Air Force base rumbled by overhead. A common occurrence and one to which I otherwise pay little attention while out observing.

The light was suddenly on the Old Scope again, and the police officer muttered something I couldn't hear clearly, something about a telescope. Louder, he said over the fence, "Sorry to bother you. Have a pleasant evening." And switching off the flashlight, he walked away up the alley. I could swear he was laughing.

I eventually learned, from the caregiver for an elderly neighbor across the alley from my house, that her charge had been the one who called the police, claiming that someone was outside with a gun, trying to shoot down planes. The elderly neighbor, who sadly suffered from a significant degree of dementia, had apparently seen me and the Old Scope.

She was very annoyed that they'd let "that terrorist" get away from them.

Given that this was just a couple of years after the 9/11 terrorist attack, I was inclined to be forgiving. I also made it a point to set up the Old Scope *before* sunset after that, so she could see exactly what I was up to. It must have worked. She never saw the terrorist again.

The other situation involved a potted plant, specifically a hanging basket with a rounded, plastic bottom, and a significantly sleep-deprived amateur astronomer. I'd taken it off its hook and set it aside so I could safely move around in the dark on the porch, without fear of a concussion when I inevitably forgot it was hanging there. I'd planned a long night, a practice session to see how I handled an all-nighter. My first ever Messier Marathon was coming up and I wanted to know how deep into the night I could go. I was well into it, observing during the wee hours of a Sunday morning, when I heard something thumping and bumping on the porch behind me.

I turned to see what was going on and saw that hanging basket pot advancing toward me across the bricks. I don't care how rational you are by the light of day, that's the sort of thing – at three o'clock in the morning and half past the last dose of caffeine –

that raises the hair on the back of your neck. I stood there for one long, awful moment, absolutely baffled by the concept of a plastic pot, trailing light-weight chains and slender branches, coming to get me. These things just don't happen outside of a cheap B-movie. The pot wobbled, turned around slowly, and moved steadily in my direction. I suddenly remembered a certain B-movie and another sleep-deprived late night from my teen years. Remembering what a fool I'd been back then, frightened out of my wits by a bullfrog in wet grass, I couldn't stand it anymore. Reaching down, I grabbed one of the chains and lifted the pot. And believe me when I say I was ready to jump – just in case.

I didn't need to. Staring up at me was the neighbor's young black cat. He meowed at me and stood up on his haunches like a little dancing bear, obviously trying to reach the pot, which he had been pushing around on the porch in his effort to mash leaves against his little furry face.

That's when I finally remembered what was growing in the basket.

Catnip.

HAPPY HALLOWEEN

Amateur astronomers are not exactly shy about sharing the view. Witness the Mars event in '03 that set me back on the path to the Moon and the stars. But not all outreach is done on such a scale, or for such a dramatic reason. Sometimes outreach happens closer to home.

At the end of October, in the first year of Newt ownership, the Cloudy Nights forum and the email service of the local club carried tales of driveway outreach, with an audience made of costumed children and their parents. Halloween, with a look through a telescope as the treat, or as an extra treat for many. It sounded as if this sort of private event was uniformly well-received by the neighbors of amateur astronomers who indulged the outreach impulse. The astronomers certainly enjoyed it. I decided to give it a try.

In 2006 opportunity and intention came together and saw me setting up the Three-legged Newt a bit before sunset on October 31st. A waxing gibbous Moon was rising, pale and mottled, in an eastern sky that was already growing darker. The sky was clear and the predicted seeing conditions were good. By the time the trick-or-treaters were out, it would be well up in the sky, ready for viewing. There was a kitchen stepladder for those lacking in altitude. I had my "outreach" eyepiece in place, one with enough field of view to encompass the Moon, enough magnification to show the more prominent lunar features well, plenty of eye relief for those wearing eyeglasses, and a low enough replacement cost that, should a mishap occur, I wouldn't feel the loss too keenly.

The sun set and night settled over a fine evening in the Old Pueblo. No breeze, balmy temperatures, and right on queue a pair of young girls, dressed as princesses and nowhere near their teens, appeared at the curb and raced to the front door. High voices shouted "Trick or Treat!" and I heard my wife making appreciative noises about their costumes. And then she pointed out the telescope and sent them my way. My first customers. Neither girl so much as hesitated, and they danced across the front yard, asking me what they would see.

"The Moon," I replied. And I pointed it out in the sky. "Have you ever seen the Moon through a telescope?" They both shook their heads, and then looked at the woman who accompanied them – most likely their mother – and she gave them an encouraging nod.

The younger of the two was boldest, and was soon on the top step of the ladder, following my instructions to look at the center of the ring I made with thumb and forefinger around the rim of the eyepiece. She never so much as hesitated and, clinging to the top rail of the ladder, leaned toward the eyepiece. I could see the light of the Moon spilling from the eyepiece onto her cheek, and then into a bright eye. She held very still for a long moment, and then very quietly said, "Wow!" It was more a breath than a word.

Older (but not by much) sister waited just long enough for her turn that she started to fidget, but eventually the little one stepped down, asking a stream of questions about mountains and craters that rather surprised me, coming from a child who had just seen the Moon through a telescope for the first time. As I answered, the other girl was being very vocal in her excitement over what she saw. And then both were chattering at Mom, one clinging to each arm as they urged her forward.

"You've *got* to see!" the older girl exclaimed.

Their mother gave me a quick look, as if asking permission, and I nodded. She took a long look, then stepped back and said, "Oh, that's so beautiful. I've never seen anything like it before!" She smiled at me and said, "Thank you for doing this."

"Most welcome," I assured her.

The evening unfolded from there, exciting, busy, and rewarding for all involved. And as luck would have it, this turned out to be one of the busiest Halloweens we'd had up to that point, living there. I learned, as the evening went on, that word of "that guy with the telescope" was spreading, and kids were asking parents and guardians to take them to our street so they could see what was going on. At times I had small crowds of children and adults at the end of my driveway. It was noisy and more than a little chaotic, and yet it never really got out of hand. Children of all ages, and in all manner of costume, received candy at our front door, and Moonlight in the driveway. They seemed equally pleased with each form of treat.

A sort of carnival atmosphere developed on the street that night, something I've not seen happen since, even on later Halloweens with the Newt in the driveway. Excited shouts rang out up and down the street, and it seemed kids were pelting about from one side of the street to the other. A band of what I took to be college students staggered up the street – there must have been more than a dozen – done up as zombies, moaning and putting on a show that was well-received. At one point, one of the neighborhood characters came by pedaling a contraption that looked like two bicycles welded together, with a mast lined by pulleys and gears rising up from the middle, just behind the rider. Attached to it were a pair of wings made of a thin metal framework. Overall, it looked like a big, slow butterfly flapping by my house, and every bit of it was lined by tiny lights winking on and off in patterns that almost made sense. It was quite an apparition when it first appeared at the corner, a few blocks to the west and near the neighborhood park. It was a while before I was sure of what I was seeing.

He slowly pedaled by us, and garnered a share of attention, but no one left the line at the eyepiece. I hope he didn't feel upstaged.

At one point, when an especially large crowd had gathered at the end of my driveway, a car slowed to a stop. The woman driving it rolled down her window and looked out as if assessing a situation, and as it turns out, that's what she was doing.

"What's wrong?" she demanded in tones eloquent of concern. "I have my phone, should I call 911?" She thought the crowd had gathered because of an accident!

"Nothing's wrong," a man's voice responded. "We're just here looking at the Moon." He was a shadow-shape in the darkness, but I could see him point to the Newt, which she only then noticed.

"Park somewhere," I suggested. "Then come back and have a look."

She drove off, and not much further up the street, turned into a driveway. A neighbor, then, and so much the better. And she did indeed come back to look at the Moon.

There were lulls, but I was never without viewers, and no few of these were kids coming back to look again, clear evidence that the right impression was being made. Most of all I was pleased by the gratitude of the parents and other guardians, who reacted to this as if it were a huge act of generosity on my part. It was a marvelous thing I was doing for the kids, I was told a number of time. You can't help feeling good, hearing such things.

One family, a nearly even mix of kids of various ages and adults, included members who were speaking French. As they took their turns at the eyepiece I found myself receiving translated questions, and waiting as answers were rendered into French. One girl in this group said nothing the entire time, and when she was at the eyepiece sighed deeply and said something in French that no one thought to interpret for me. It was clearly a happy thing, whatever the words meant. One of the adults had appointed herself the guardian of courtesy, and had admonished the kids so often to say "thank you," that when she spoke to this small slip of a girl I just knew that's what was said, even though this time it was in French.

The little girl said nothing. Standing on the top step of the ladder she turned, leaned forward, and very solemnly kissed me on the cheek.

All of those who took a look were impressed by the Newt, which cuts an imposing figure. And that impression led several parents, suddenly faced with children who thought it would be ever so cool to have a telescope of their own, to ask pointed questions about prices. The cost of my rig raised eyebrows – and the Newt is anything but "high end." I was quick to point out that this was no beginner's set-up, and there were easier ways to bring a telescope into the family. I made sure they knew how to find their way to Starizona. This was an oft-repeated conversation, but one example stands out above the others in my memory.

She was in her early teens, with two younger brothers in tow, and her parents hovering in the background, letting the kids have their experience with as little intervention as could be safely managed. All three children were enthusiastic and, led by older sister, started asking very good questions about telescopes in general. I answered to the best of my ability. In time, they moved off, but the young lady returned half an hour or so later to take another look. The questions then were all about the costs of such things and about sources for telescopes and accessories. Her siblings were working the other side of the street, but she was no longer interested in candy. This kid was serious, and already fairly knowledgeable about matters astronomical. I told her I'd started with a much smaller instrument and had only recently moved up to the Newt. When she finally left – it had gotten late and things were settling down – she did so with a thoughtful look on her face. Perhaps I should say – calculating.

The family went on up the street, and things grew steadily quieter. My wife appeared to inform me that she was shutting down her part of the operation, having run out of candy to hand out. I was exhausted, but brimming with stories to tell. I waited a little longer, but no one was out, and I started taking things apart. Ten minutes after I'd begun the tear-down process, the father of that teenage girl appeared.

"Oh, good, you're still here," he said. "My daughter wants to get into this," and he waved a hand at the Newt.

"Seeing the Moon this way has that effect on kids," I replied.

"No, she was like that before we got here," he said. "She's serious."

He asked questions, and I answered. The man took my suggestion of an 8-inch Dobsonian mounted reflector under advisement and accepted my email address, in case more questions occurred. Then he shook my hand and said, "This is a great thing you did for the kids. Thanks for that." And walked away.

I never heard from him. I have no idea what came of all that. One can only hope.

I've done the Halloween thing a few times since that night, but none of those experiences match that one. It was insane, it was intense, it was chaotic at times, but it was more fun than I've ever had sharing the view before or since.

Happy Halloween, indeed!

MARATHON

Charles Messier's famous catalog has become something of a rite-of-passage for amateur astronomers. As a teenager, I had an idea that those objects marked with "M" followed by a number were important, but the few references I had available to me were less than explicit regarding who Messier was, why he made the catalog, and what this venerable list meant to astronomy hobbyists. This all changed very quickly when I became immersed in the online amateur astronomy community. I was quickly up to speed on these matters, and was soon hunting down Messier objects both at home and under darker skies.

Even before I purchased the Three-legged Newt, I came across stories of something called a Messier Marathon. It seemed there was a window of time, each spring, when it was possible to observe almost every Messier object between sunset and sunrise. Many people seemed drawn to the challenge, but at first it really didn't appeal to me. Oddly enough this was because I'm a birdwatcher. My wife and I share a general interest in the natural world, and in our travels together through the American Southwest always haul a box full of field guides and other references with us. The birds we encounter take up the most time, and are usually what we travel to see. We keep lists and take notes, but never just check species off a list, a common approach to birdwatching. We prefer to take our time, study the birds we find, and try to witness and understand something of their behavior. As a result, in places where some birders will cover a lot of ground and generate impressive lists, we're likely to go half the distance, and see fewer species while coming back with stories of what we saw the birds do. One of our favorite birding techniques involves sitting down in a spot where a resource such as water is likely to attract birds – and wait.

My observing habits parallel those birding and nature study habits. After I've found an object, I'm likely to study it for a long time, just as my wife and I will watch a bird for a while before moving on up the trail. It just seems, well, natural to me, in both cases. The idea of rushing from one object to the next all night long sounded a bit ridiculous, so at first I dismissed it.

And yet, as winter gave way to spring and people started talking about marathon plans, I found myself attracted by their enthusiasm. It wasn't observing, not in the usual sense, but it wasn't really the list-ticking habit I dislike in impatient birdwatchers, either. It was more like a sporting event, a test of skill and endurance. I started checking the reference material that has come into being to support this annual event, and listened to the stories told by fellow enthusiasts.

I'd already decided to attend the All-Arizona Messier Marathon in the spring of 2005, having enjoyed that brief experience of observing from the Arizona City site the previous October. But I initially intended to be there for the dark skies and the camaraderie, not to "run" the marathon. By the time the appointed weekend in March arrived, I'd decided to see for myself what it was all about.

Once again I drove a rented SUV out into the desert, first north to Casa Grande and then doubling back south – more or less – through Arizona City to the All-Arizona Star Party site of that time. It was March 12th and due to some hassles picking up the rental, I arrived later in the afternoon than I'd intended. While that late arrival limited time for setting up and socializing, it also allowed me to avoid being out in a place utterly lacking in shade on a day of unusually hot weather, for the season.

Unfortunately, it also meant that I never had a chance to rest up from the day's preparations before setting up, doing the meeting and greeting, and then leaping into the event at sunset – which came all too soon, that time of year.

But I was there, in a flat field now covered with filaree and some sort of low-growing amaranth, and not nearly as dusty as it had been before. The winter's rains had been unusually generous to the desert, supporting a lush growth of vegetation that made the scene less harsh than it had been the previous autumn. The plants also reduced the amount of dust brought up by the inevitable breezes that seem the norm for that area.

As the sun sank into the dusty western sky, I joined a group of TAAA members and set up for the night, then went around the field meeting up with people from the Cloudy Nights forum, most of whom lived in the Phoenix metro area. (I caught up with Ron, who delivered an altered and less dangerous wooden observing chair. It was the object of much attention on the part of other attendees.) At sunset everyone gathered for a reading of the rules, and to pick up copies of the official checklist, after which we wished each other luck, and waited for it to get dark enough to bag the first objects.

The western sky was decorated by a brilliant two-day-old crescent Moon. Bright as it was, it had little influence on my inability to find M77 and M74, galaxies in Cetus and Pisces respectively. They were expected to be difficult, being right on the edge of twilight and very low in the west, and while some folks got them, for many of us the brightness of the twilight sky was too much. I made the attempt, then let those two sink into the horizon haze as I sought more objects. I never put the Moon in the scope, which is unusual for me, but just after sunset did take a brief and uninspiring look at Mercury, since it was as well-placed for viewing as it ever gets.

My true marathon efforts began with putting M45 in the field of view of the widest field eyepiece I had at that time – the 25mm Plössl that came with the Newt. In the hour that followed, I spotted eight objects, which from the comments I overheard around me was a very slow rate of discovery. Part of the challenge I faced was working with a much busier sky than I was accustomed to. There's a concept for you, being slowed down on a Messier Marathon because there were too many stars overhead! My success rate did increase as I worked, but that slow start would take its toll, especially when I tackled the galaxies of Virgo. This was a special challenge for me, because until that night I'd never ventured into that corner of the universe. First time galaxy-hunting in Virgo and Coma Berenices on a Messier Marathon? I don't recommend it!

In the end I was only able to be sure of a handful of the galaxies in that part of the sky, and I finally decided to stop struggling with those particular faint fuzzies in order to move on to other objects rising steadily into the eastern sky. Few experiences, in that first year with the Newt, made it clearer that I had a long way yet to go up the learning curve.

I still stuck with the official list, which was more or less ordered according to when an object would be high enough in the east to be glimpsed at least. Still, I was slow enough at it that as often as not an object was near the meridian before I caught up with it. I kept telling myself I was doing fine for a first-timer, especially since I'd only observed a handful of Messier objects "officially," to that point. The overwhelming majority of the items on the list I knew only from what I'd read in books, and my object location skills with that telescope were not quite a year in the making. Taking all of that into account, I was actually doing pretty well!

And I kept telling myself that as the night grew older and colder, and stars slid inexorably from east to west, carrying my quarries with them. Yes, it had its frustrating moments.

I stopped from time to time to eat something and drink water and the occasional caffeinated beverage. Though I was tired, I felt alert enough to keep going. It had been recommended that I take a nap in the middle of the night to restore myself, but I knew by that point that if I went to sleep, the next star I saw would be the Sun. So I stayed the course.

Now and then I walked around the field to stretch my legs and back, talking to other observers, many of whom were running the marathon. I wasn't the only one struggling, it seemed, though most of those I spoke to were much farther down the list than I was. I took those walks less often as the night rolled on. Foolish, I know, especially under the circumstances, but fatigue was rendering me thin-skinned and irritable. It didn't help that the two participants nearest me were calling out object numbers as they bagged them at a rate I couldn't hope to match.

That such things were getting under my skin was surely an indication of how close to the end of my endurance I was, by the time the chilly early morning hours rolled in.

Although I felt some frustration, there was still an element of wonder to it all. The quiet desert at night, the perfectly clear sky above, and from time to time a moment of amazement as I located something spectacular. The Swan Nebula (M17) really did look like a bird on a pond, though it brought to mind a cormorant instead of a swan. I saw a hint of spiral arms in the Whirlpool Galaxy (M51). M13, the great globular cluster in Hercules, was simply mind-blowing in a dark sky. The planetary nebula in M46 was plain to see. And yes, I was many times distracted by wonders seen for the first time. That didn't help my pace at all, I'm sure!

There was also the peculiar moaning sound I kept hearing, every time a gentle night breeze swept across the desert. It took a ridiculous amount of time to realize that the odd and oddly distracting sound was coming from the Newt, as the wind blew across the open end of the tube.

In the end, I didn't go the distance. Sometime after 3:00am (my notes say 3:35am), I found myself standing there beside the scope, suddenly very confused. I'd paused to eat the remains of one of the sandwiches I'd brought with me, taken a few deep breaths to steady myself, and check which object was next. By the time I turned from my chart table to the Newt, I couldn't remember what object it was, or where to point the scope. There was an odd sensation; my head swam for a moment, and I was standing with my hands on the tube with no idea how to use the Newt. I'm pretty sure I was, for a moment, asleep standing up.

Enough was enough. I leveled the tube, capped it and removed the eyepiece, capping the focuser as well. Locking the tube in place in its "resting" position – pointed north at a shallow angle – I crawled into the car, curled up on the pads that had cushioned the Newt on the trip in, and fell asleep for real.

I slept for three or four hours and awoke to a clear, cold desert morning, surrounded by the waking dead. Not that I was in such great shape myself, you understand. There were smiles and some laughter as people started to pack things up. Everyone who had done the marathon had a bit of paperwork to do, turning in their results to the event coordinator. I put away my gear, then sat down to count my final total for my own records before turning in the form. To my amazement, I'd managed to find 84 of the 109 possible Messier objects for that night, for a success rate of 77%. When it was made known this was my first attempt, hearty congratulations were bestowed.

I felt pretty damned good, and was more than willing to join several fellow amateur astronomers for breakfast in Arizona City. It was a fine ending to a grand experience, and the coffee and omelet (mostly the coffee) probably saved my life on the drive home.

During subsequent marathons I've scored better than one hundred objects. It's been a while since I did one of these. As I've grown older, I've found myself less and less able to endure all-nighters. That's too bad, really, but at least I can say I've had that experience, and it was a lot of fun.

OBSERVATIONS

‡

A NOTE ON THE GEAR

Before sharing specific eyepiece experiences, allow me to share the eyepieces – among other items – in a manner of speaking.

The purchase of the Three-legged Newt was followed by a few years of research, experimentation, and spending. Emphasis on the word "spending." There eventually came a time when gear stopped accumulating. I had atlases that suited my needs, along with eyepieces, filters, a Barlow lens, and a coma corrector. For much of my observing career, since sometime in 2008, I've used the following without significant changes or additions. I'm listing things here so I don't need to reiterate ad nauseam in the chapters that follow. (I do have eyepieces other than those listed, but they are seldom used with the Three-legged Newt, these days, and do not come into play in the accounts that follow.)

- SkyView Pro 8 – an 8 inch (203mm) Newtonian on an equatorial mount
- Telrad & 9x50 Optical Finderscope
- Orion Stratus Eyepieces: 21mm, 17mm, 13mm, 8mm, 5mm, 3.5mm
- Paragon 40mm Eyepiece
- TeleVue Paracorr Type 2
- Variable Polarizing Filter
- OIII filter (1.25 and 2 inch)
- Orion Ultrablock Narrowband Filter (1.25 and 2 inch)
- 8x42 Celestron Noble Binoculars
- Assorted Observing Aides (chair, tables, red light, collimation tools, etc.)

Use of a Type 2 Paracorr increases the magnification of an eyepiece by 1.15x (15%) – and with the Stratus eyepieces I almost always use the Paracorr. This leads to some rather funky magnification numbers, which for my eyepieces are as follows:

- Stratus 21mm – 55x
- Stratus 17mm – 68x
- Stratus 13mm – 89x
- Stratus 8mm – 144x
- Stratus 5mm – 230x
- Stratus 3.5mm – 329X
- Paragon 40mm – 29x

In addition to the hardware, there's a still-expanding library of reference material that includes atlases, observing guides, and general works on astronomy.

I had my reasons for making the choices I did, when buying astronomy gear. Suffice to say this collection works for me. YMMV, your mileage may vary, as they say on the forum.

THREE EVENINGS IN DECEMBER

Since my teenage astronomy phase, I've rarely managed to set up a telescope and observe two nights running. Growing up, there were runs of glorious summer nights when this could happen, and I have fond memories of being out there under the stars night after night several nights in a row. When you're fourteen years old you have that kind of energy, though truth be told, there were plenty of "next days" when, chores completed, I grabbed rod and reel and headed for Hickory Creek more to catch up on sleep than to catch fish.

Being all grown up now, I'm lucky if I can run Friday and Saturday nights back-to-back. In fact, since acquiring the Three-legged Newt, and except for the occasion that prompted this essay, I have done back-to-back observing sessions only during the rare All-Arizona Star Parties during which I could get out on a Friday afternoon. For most of those events, when they were still within reach, I just did Saturday night. I can count these occasions on one hand. Vacations happen, but I'm generally busy doing other things during such breaks and astronomy isn't usually a priority. The winter break I get every holiday season, working for the University of Arizona, provides a span of time in which I *should* be able to string a couple of nights together, but in the years since I staged my stargazing comeback, I've been lucky if the winter weather gives me even one cloudless night. Having three evenings in a row in which to indulge myself in this pastime would count as little more than a pipe dream.

And yet during the 2008 iteration of the University's winter break, something amazing happened. The usual winter storm system that always seems to roll through Arizona right in the middle of the break, did so at the very start of it, for a change – just in time for Christmas, bringing snow to northern parts of the state and pleasing children there no end, I'm sure. The weather system that filled in behind it was beautiful, almost spring-like, in my half of the state. Transparent skies and predictions of good seeing dominated the Clear Sky Chart. In fact, on the 28th of December, 2008, I found myself checking the CSC and seeing nothing but deep blue in all the blocks for the next three nights. Rare enough, all by itself, but this was happening while I was on vacation!

I don't set the Newt up without a clear set of objectives; that's just the way I work. Now I suddenly found myself with three nights in a row, right there for the taking, and to take them I would need a plan quickly, for that first night, at least. On impulse I pulled out my planisphere and the binder in which I keep printed copies of Tom Trusock's *Small Wonders* series, published once upon a time on the Cloudy Nights website. (It's still archived there.) I looked through the binder, earmarked constellations appropriate for that season, and there was my observing plan. All I needed at that point was the early winter sunset.

28 December 2008

My intention was to pick a constellation and observe everything in it that appeared in its *Small Wonders* installment, but in my hasty planning, I underestimated how much new growth our robust mesquite trees had put on in the previous year. A couple of the constellations I meant to cover were completely lost in the trees.

I started with the constellation Andromeda, and for not the first time observed Almach (gamma Andromedae), the double star alleged to give Albireo a run for its money in terms of color contrast. It's a pretty pair, but to my mind it does no such thing. Splitting it was easy enough, but the color contrast really didn't stand out until I bumped up the magnification. Many authors have noted that color contrasts can be enhanced by an increase in magnification, and that proved to be the case for Almach. At 55x it was obvious the components weren't the same color; at 144x what those colors were became clearer. The primary star had a distinct ruddy-golden hue, while the companion star was a spark of pale, ashen blue. Many authors call the companion star "white." This is not the first time my observation of a double star has not precisely matched what others have recorded, and this is not unusual among astronomers in general. I only worry about it if other writers see something as orange, and I see blue. At that point I make sure I'm looking at the correct binary star.

At my very first dark-sky star party I made the acquaintance of a galaxy popularly known as

Mirach's Ghost (NGC 404), Mirach being another name for beta Andromedae. Even in a large Dobsonian, on the night the Ghost and I first met, it was a grey smudge that could easily be mistaken for glare from the second magnitude star near it. On that first occasion, my fellow club member nudged the star out of the field of view, making the distant galactic smudge more obvious for what it was. This was all through a much larger reflector than the Newt, but intrigued by what I'd seen (and knowing now where and how to look), I tried to track it down for myself and succeeded. This pleased me no end. Even more pleasing was the discovery this night that I can see NGC 404 from my back yard. At 55x it was hard to tell if I actually saw the galaxy, or was tricking myself because I knew where it should be. At 144x, however, it was definitely there, and popped out clearly when I used averted vision. Of course, under suburban conditions (with the glare of the bright star nearby), I was doing little more than detecting the pale glow of the distant galaxy, even when I moved Mirach out of the field of view. On the other hand, observations I've made of this galaxy from dark-sky sites are not exactly rich with details. But it was quite distinctly there, and no doubt about it, and so I listed the observation as a success. The observation interested me, even though the galaxy truly was faint and fuzzy. The star Almach was, on the scale of the grander universe, right there with me in my back yard with me. I was looking past a near neighbor, something on the order of ten million light-years away, to an object far brighter than an individual star, and yet so muted by dust and distance that it could be nicknamed the ghost of that nearer star.

Such contemplations, by themselves, often keep me up at the eyepiece, deep into the night.

Messier 31 is an old friend, the first galaxy outside the Milky Way I ever observed through a telescope. I can find and observe the core region of M31 from my back yard, but other details generally elude me. And yet I usually take a look, when it's available. The fuzzy star-like image of M32, resembling nothing so much as a really faint globular cluster, was easy to pick out. M110, on the other hand, was less than obvious at first glance. With averted vision and some patience I could see it. For all that it is technically the brighter of the two, I actually found it easier to make out NGC 404 (Mirach's Ghost) than M110 – go figure.

My next target was the open cluster NGC 752 which, when I found it, proved difficult to see clearly. This puzzled me at first, since I'd observed the cluster before from my back yard. Stepping back and looking up the length of the OTA, I discovered that I was trying to observe it through the outer twigs of a mesquite tree. In astronomy as in fishing, there always seems to be one that gets away. More than one, in this case, since the *Small Wonders* article in the binder discussed more objects in Andromeda than I was able to see through the tree.

Auriga, in the meantime, was well up into the eastern sky, an area that I can observe easily from the backyard location. Capella (alpha Aurigae) never fails to draw my eye, and is discussed in *Small Wonders* Auriga, so of course I centered it in my low-power "finder" eyepiece. Capella isn't a visual double, has no 'ghosts,' and isn't part of a cluster. It's "just" a star – a very bright and beautiful star. What I saw was a blazing point of molten silver, with that breath-catching purity of color only starlight can possess. Such a sight is well worth the time spent.

The first *Small Wonders* DSO I decided to go after in Auriga would have been a new one for me. I say 'would have been,' because for some reason I just could not convince myself that there was a star cluster where the charts say NGC 1857 is supposed to be. I'm reasonably sure I got the position right, but nothing really stood out to my eye. This happens, from time to time, and for a variety of reasons. I could have tried to out-stubborn the situation, but in every observing session the clock, quite literally, is ticking. Instead of spending too much time doggedly pursuing an object that I just was not finding (or seeing – an important distinction), I made a note to try again later, at a darker site, to see if that made a difference.

On to another new (to me) object, NGC 1907, in the vicinity of M38. This time it was quite clear that there was an object present in the form of a faint grey patch of light just visible at 55x. I worked my way up through the range of magnifications available to me and had a reasonably good look at a few tiny stars embedded in a mottling of not quite resolved starlight. The few stars I could resolve were seen using averted vision, and took some time and watching to detect. Going by *Small Wonders*, I was doing well to get that far! I was left with the distinct impression that this cluster was another object worth revisiting when I find myself under dark skies. My observing lists for such excursions are often a mix of faint nebulae, galaxies, and items such as NGC 1907 that give me hints of greater detail through the suburban glow.

The time and energy I could spare for this last-minute, unexpected observing session were running out. It had been a busy day, I'd started out a bit tired, and now the chill of the desert winter was settling in, aided by a light breeze. It was time to go in, open a few books, and address the mystery of NGC 1857. It was my intention to be more productive the second night out.

29 December 2008

NGC 1857 did not elude me a second night. Having used several resources to familiarize myself with the cluster and its location, I went out a bit better prepared for the search. In the *Small Wonders* piece on Auriga, an asterism reminiscent of Cassiopeia is mentioned. I aimed the Telrad in the right spot and went to the optical finder, but saw a few stars that didn't shape up as expected. From what I'd read, I decided to trust the Telrad, and go to the eyepiece. This time I had the lowest power, widest field eyepiece in my kit in place (29x and better than 2°) and when I focused it – there was the mini-Cassiopeia asterism mentioned (and illustrated) in *Small Wonders*.

Using that asterism to point the way I could, at low magnification, see a haze of faint light roughly associated with (if not centered on) a pair of stars, one brighter and considerably redder than the other. With increased magnification (89x) I could just make out a sprinkling of faint stars in the vicinity of that pale orange star. More magnification (144x was as high as I went on this) made the gathering of stars more obviously a cluster, with numerous relatively faint pinpricks of light visible in the vicinity of the brighter duo I used to zero in on my target. There were elusive hints of structure to this demure stellar gathering, as if the stars were not arranged uniformly across that little patch of space. It proved a star cluster of subtle beauty, and well worth the effort to finally find it.

I celebrated my little breakthrough by visiting a

set of old friends, the big three of Messier open clusters in Auriga: M37, M36, and M38. I started with M37, an open cluster of fairly bright stars grouped into pairs and trios that are themselves gathered into short, curved arcs. The brightest star is almost but not quite centered in the cluster, and has a gold cast to it. I seem to recall reading somewhere that this might be a foreground star, and not part of the cluster proper. Like the other Messier clusters in Auriga, and open clusters anywhere, it pays to play with magnification and see what works on a given night. Tonight I had my best look at M37 at 89x. The seeing (and to a certain extent the transparency) on one night might support 144x with the Newt, but next time out things get a bit fuzzy above 89x. Like any deep-sky object, M37 was worth a long look, and I took one. The longer I look at such an object, the more structured and detailed it appears. Obvious first impressions fade and things not immediately apparent are noticed.

When I was finally able to tear myself away from that open cluster, I nudged the Newt a bit west and found M36 easily enough. Once again, 89x proved to be the power of choice. M36 looks looser, coarser, and more spread out than M37, with a dozen or more fairly bright, and uniformly bright to my eye, stars arranged in pairs and trios. These arrangements are in scattered clumps rather than loose chains. The area behind these most prominent members was a field rich with stars that gradually blended out into the star field around the cluster. Another nudge brought M38 into the field of view; since it had been best two times out of three, I left the same eyepiece in place. M38 is the most subtle of this trio. Its individual stars are not as bright as those of its near neighbors, but seem to me to be more numerous and closely packed. It's a quiet- looking cluster with curved chains of starlight and something of a dim lane running more or less through the middle. I always get a feeling of great distance between M38 and my eye, as if something much brighter had sunk to a great depth in dark water. Curiously enough, it really isn't that much further from my eye than the other two.

NGC 1664, another of the open clusters discussed in *Small Wonders* for Auriga, is one of many such objects that have me wondering how its discoverers figured out it was an open cluster. In my preferred finder eyepiece (55x), NGC 1664 didn't exactly stand out from the star field. With the help of the description in *Small Wonders* and the use of a wider field of view (29x), I was able to finally see that the very loose and scattered splash of fairly uniform stars actually constituted an object. It was a pretty view through the eyepiece, but an impatient observer, scanning a bit too quickly, might not realize a cluster had passed through the view. A pair of brighter stars flanking the cluster helped me to make sure that I was looking at the right place. Once I was acquainted with the star cluster, it was easy enough to observe at 55x. After looking at it for a moment my eye picked out the shape of a stingray gliding through dark waters, its slightly curved tail trailing behind. Afterward I discovered that this cluster is sometimes called The Kite Cluster. That I saw the animal I did may have something to do with who I'd been cheering for in the 2008 World Series.

Small Wonders lists the planetary nebula IC 2149 as a challenge object, and given my suburban location, that seemed likely to prove an understatement. I decided to give it a try all the same. Ironically, it proved far less of a challenge than NGC 1857, at least in terms of finding it. Having 8 inches of aperture at my disposal helped, of course, revealing it as an "unfocused" star even in a low power eyepiece. By the time I worked my way up to 230x it was obvious this was not a star, but the puffed-up remains of one. I couldn't help thinking Herschel's descriptive name for this sort of object is very appropriate. With an OIII filter, I found myself looking at a slightly oblate cloud of light, the long axis such as it was running more-or-less east-west. I couldn't see much more than that, but being able to track it down and see it from a moderately light-polluted back yard was a very satisfying experience.

My intention for the evening was to "finish" the list of *Small Wonders* in Auriga, and I had done so. It had been a fairly long session and the night was anything but young – actually, you could say the morning was on the youthful side – and if it seems that's a lot of time for only a few objects, call me a slow observer. When I get something in the eyepiece I don't hurry on to the next target. But before I called it quits, I put the eyepiece with the widest field of view and lowest power (29x) in the focuser and spent some time with M45 and M42. The seeing was once again very good, and so the bright blue-white gems of the Seven Sisters burned with exceptional clarity. The cluster fit into the field of view with room to spare, a splendid sight, Tennyson's fireflies free of their "silver braid". A few moments before deciding to take in the view, I'd been contemplating an end to the evening. I put that ending off quite a while.

That generous field of view also allowed me to view the entire scene of M42 and M43 at a glance, from NGC 1981 to iota Orionis. M42 was a small, grey, bird-like shape in a space darkened by an OIII filter, a bird in flight making a tight turn by partly closing one wing, with a tiny cluster of diamonds at its throat. The diamonds are spilling away. I could see a couple of them rolling down the closed wing.

And with that, I packed it up and called it a night, for all that it was early morning.

30 December 2008

After allowing myself to sleep in and then taking it easy all day, I felt rested and ready for a third night of observing, and was able to go on a little later into the night. However, I did not get to it as early as I would have liked, and so missed the chance to explore Perseus as I'd originally planned. Those trees again, with inconveniently placed branches. The only item listed in *Small Wonders* that I observed in Perseus was M34. As was true of the Messiers in Auriga last night, this is a cluster I have seen several times before. I frequently revisit objects because, in astronomy at least, familiarity breeds understanding rather than contempt. I used the single-degree eyepiece, and the relatively wide field of view made it obvious that this was an object, an aggregation of fairly bright stars, even if it is a rather widely spread aggregation. The stars seemed to me to be arranged in sets of widely spaced pairs. This is a fairly bright, if not exactly crowded cluster, one I've found easy to at least detect using my 8x42 birding binoculars. I'm told some people can pick it out naked-eye at a dark site, a trick I have not yet been able to pull off.

That was as far as I could go with Perseus, for the night, so I shifted my attention to the constellation that always held me spellbound as a small boy, venturing out on dark and frosty winter nights in Illinois – Orion.

I would have put the Newt on alpha Orionis (Betelgeuse) even if the star had not been included in the *Small Wonders* write-up. As I said on the first day of this brief observing trilogy, the purity of light and color of bright stars holds a powerful attraction. In the eyepiece Betelgeuse looked more golden than red to me, an effect that was more apparent if I increased the magnification. Strangely enough, it looked redder in the binoculars than it did naked-eye or through an eyepiece stuck into the Newt. Ruddy orange with eyes and telescope, more distinctly red in the binoculars. I've yet to find an explanation for why that should be.

From there I went to beta Orionis, brilliant Rigel, and absorbed photons of pure blue-white fire for a change of pace. Conditions were good enough that I hoped I'd see the companion of this double star. I thought I could make the split at 89x, but was quite sure of it at 144x. The magnitude contrast between Rigel and the tiny, faint spark beside it was profound (0.13 vs 6.7). There did not seem to be much of a color contrast, the companion seeming white to my eye, but in the glare of Rigel it's hard to be sure.

Another double that I enjoy revisiting in Orion, and that *Small Wonders* quite properly lists, is delta Orionis – Mintaka. I've looked at and split this double star with every telescope I can recall owning over the years, and many of those telescopes of childhood were of pretty poor quality. This is an easy double, but no less attractive for all of that. For one thing the setting, in a wide-field eyepiece, is quite pretty. The pair itself consists of a roughly second magnitude star of clean white hue, with a chilly bluish sixth magnitude companion. I never went higher than 55x; I found myself enjoying the wider view too much, and the star was split handily enough at that magnification.

Collinder (Cr) 69 came next on the *Small Wonders* hit parade, a cluster that I've pretty much ignored over the years, outside of the occasional sweep with binoculars. In fact, I'm not certain I knew for sure, before I started working on Collinder's Catalog (the link to my weblog at the end of this book will take you to that publication), that this was a cluster at all. I first observed it as an object more than a year ago using a 102mm refractor. Using my lowest magnification, I was able to do Cr 69 justice in the Newt. The initial impression is of a triangular asterism formed by phi 1, phi 2, and lambda Orionis, the last being a moderately close (and pretty) double star, also named Meissa. A third faint star gives it the look of a triple star, but none of the references I own include it as a part of that system. Phi 2 Orionis, it turns out, isn't part of Cr 69, and removing it from consideration left me with a sort of strung-out, curved star cluster, two bright stars with three more evenly spaced but not exactly lined up between them. There was a loose scatter of faint stars just to the east of those forming the line, and these are, to the best of my knowledge, members of the cluster. This isn't a particularly bright or rich cluster, but it certainly is an oddly shaped one. In volume one of the Night Sky Observer's Guide (NSOG) the suggestion is made to use an OIII filter and averted vision, when using a telescope of at least 8 inches aperture on this object, to pick up a haze of nebulosity around the brighter stars. I tried this, but no such luck.

No eyepiece I own could, combined with the Newt, do justice to Cr 70, the star cluster that exists in and around Orion's Belt. Binoculars do the trick, though. I've always known that the binocular view of the Belt was spectacular, but I didn't always know that this was an open star cluster. In my 8x42 binoculars, the Belt Cluster is a star field to rival that of the alpha Persei Association, and like the latter cluster there is little, in a suburban sky, that provides to the naked eye any hint that such an assemblage of stars exists. The first time I looked at the sky around the Belt through binoculars I experienced a sort of Galileo moment, in which a set of lenses revealed to me that there was more here than meets the eye. The three bright stars of Orion's belt are suddenly the brightest members of a swarm of hundreds of bright stars of various magnitudes. It's a dramatic and, when seen for the first time, surprising transformation.

As I surveyed the stars of the Belt Cluster, the nightlife of Tucson made itself known. No, not the college students (all safely home for the holidays) – coyotes. From somewhere north in the not-quite darkness I heard them singing. They were probably in the bed of the Rillito River, a couple of miles to the north. I always pause when I hear them, marveling that such wildness could live in the city. Hearing them in the night is a blessing. When I'm out with the Newt and *don't* hear them, the night somehow feels incomplete.

NGC 1662 was another object new to my experience. As discussed in *Small Wonders*, this is a cluster you need to make sure of in your finder scope. With just a Telrad and a bit of sweeping, you might lose this one in the busy star fields around it. Low power and a wide field of view, yet again, did the trick. I found this to be an odd little cluster, a sort of knotted string of stars that quickly trailed off and blended in with the background. And yet it was an appealing object, and one I have on my list of objects to revisit.

Of course, I spent a fair amount of my time that night (most of my time, actually) looking at M42 and its neighbors through various eyepieces, with and without an OIII filter. I sketched a variety of these views, but found that none of the sketches really worked out as I hoped. There was something about the amount of detail that came to me as I sat there that rendered the sharpest pencil I own little more than a blunt instrument. And yet, the next morning the sketches clearly served their purpose, which was to stimulate my memory and bring the wonder of the view the night before back to me. Visual observers who clutch pencils in the night know what I mean.

The seeing was once again quite good, so I decided to try catching the E and F stars of the Trapezium. The basic quartet was no challenge and I took some time to appreciate them before increasing the magnification. While doing so I was startled to see a tiny star seem to appear from within the nebular glow and zip smoothly away. It took me a moment to realize it must have been a satellite that passed across the nebula unnoticed until it emerged, so to speak, into the darker sky just off the Fish's Mouth. With a quiet laugh, I pushed the magnification a bit more and at 144x had little trouble picking out the E star. Now and then the F component of this marvelous multiple star trembled into view. At 230x both the fainter stars were visible all of the time. I've read various accounts of the colors of the stars in the 'Trap,' but all of them look bluish or white to my eye.

I spent some time on NGC 1981 and the nearby nebulae NGC 1973, NGC 1975, and NGC 1977, mostly experimenting with filters to see if I could detect any nebulosity at all. I've sometimes been surprised by what I can do and see from my backyard site. I had some interesting views of the region, but didn't really pull out any glimpses of cosmic cloudiness. Perhaps another time, or at a different location – someday.

And it works that way, from one celestial object to the next. At any given location you win some and lose some. I have only ever seen M78 from a dark site; my past efforts to find this reflection nebula from the back yard have been complete misses. Since it was on the Small Wonders list, and conditions were so good, I thought I'd give it another try. The two stars that give the nebula a ghostly face-like illusion were easy enough to find, and if I used averted vision there was a trace of nebulosity around them, but no view (filtered or not) really gave a clear impression of what was there. M78 is definitely a nebula that shows poorly if there is much light pollution around. The same is very true of NGC 2071, which should have been in the same field of view with a couple of the eyepieces I used. Of this nebula not a trace was to be seen. Also missing in action was the planetary nebula on the *Small Wonders* list, NGC 2022. I know I had it in the field of view, but could never be certain that I actually saw it.

Win some and lose some. When the sky is clear and you've got the time, wherever you are, you take a look and see what you can see.

JEWELS IN DARK SETTINGS, TWO BY TWO

Spring is not a season that presents a lot of deep-sky objects to the slice of sky I can see from my tree-crowded back yard. There are spring galaxies galore, to be sure, but with an average naked-eye limiting magnitude of 4.5 and Sky Quality Meter reading of 18.64 magnitudes per arc second, distant galaxies can be a bit unrewarding. Or invisible. A clear, Moonless spring night where I live might then seem to be a night of limited opportunities. That's true only if you dismiss an entire class of deep-sky objects, and who in their right mind would do that? I'm talking about double stars, of course.

Double and multiple star observing was something that caught my fancy as a teenager, and back then they, and the Moon, made up the majority of my observations. The interest was in part due to the fact that this class of objects includes many star systems that are perfect for observing with the small refractor I had at that time. It was also due in part to the one solid reference I had available to me then, the venerable

Field Book of the Skies by William Tyler Olcott. There was such an emphasis on double stars in that book that, frankly, I thought this is just what astronomers did!

So double stars have been a major interest for me all along, and when I bought the Three-legged Newt I saw no reason to change this. The extra aperture, with the greater resolving power it provided, merely expanded the catalog of available doubles, and I was soon taking advantage of that extended reach.

An interest in double stars gives me an excuse to set up at home on a fine spring evening, even when there's no Moon to watch. This particular occasion started with a perfectly clear April sky that, after sunset, ran from pale blue in the low west to about as dark as it gets in Tucson, off over the Rincon Mountains to the east. When I went out, The brightest stars already burned brightly in the twilight, including my first target, alpha Geminorum.

I'd looked at and split Castor a few times by then, using the Newt, but that's never seemed to me a reason not to look again. This time of year, the Twins are standing more or less upright high in the west, making anything within that constellation easy pickings for the Newt. At 55x the pair formed a bright, white oblong, like a star that would not quite focus. Castor C was a pale speck to the south-southeast. At 89x I had a clean split, but the view was much improved by increasing the magnification to 144x. Two pure white stars of equal (second) magnitude dominated the view, close together, a matching pair of diamonds in the night. I pushed the magnification to 230x, which did nothing to improve the view, but did serve to illustrate that the seeing conditions were very good.

I took a long look at Castor C, trying to detect the "pale lilac" color I've seen mentioned regarding this component of the set, but saw only a very faint white star that had something of the quality of frost on a window in winter.

On the list I'd drawn up earlier in the day, delta Geminorum came next. It was no challenge to find, being visible to the naked eye in the darkening sky. At 55x I saw a whitish star with a bit of warmth to it, but no hint at all that this was a double star. At 89x I could just detect the tiny spark that was the companion star, but 144x brought it into plain sight. The difference in magnitude between them was considerable, third magnitude for the main star, eighth for the companion. In terms of color contrast, the bright primary star of the pair looked a touch warmer than pure white to me, lacking the diamond-bright purity of Castor, while the companion star was a spark of palest blue. These two are pretty close together, all of seven arc seconds apart, and on a night of lesser seeing they might have been a bit of a challenge, even for the Newt. Tonight there was no difficulty in examining both members of this pair, more evidence that this was a good night to be at the eyepiece.

It was a pleasant evening, weather-wise, into the bargain. Not long after the sun set I found a light sweat jacket comforting, but it never grew chilly enough for more than that. The breeze, when it came, was refreshing and scented by the sweet alyssum growing in the garden beside which I observe. Ah, spring in the desert, when the evening is cool and geckos get frisky. Yes, geckos, several of which were on the wall of the house beside me. They knew it was spring, to judge by the quiet chirps and barks they emitted, and by the general scampering about as they worked out who owned what part of the wall. I have to be careful packing up at the end of a session, this time of year, or I risk bringing one or two into the house with me. There they would become cat toys, a cruel fate and one I don't want on my conscience. I am very careful to leave my tiny neighbors on their wall, where they belong.

My next target was 38 Geminorum, a star that was just a bit too faint to pick out with my eyes alone. Using the stars that *could* be seen to guide me, and a pair of binoculars, I used the charts I have to familiarize myself with the region around 38 Gem. I looked for patterns, shapes, or asterisms that would show up in the finder scope, preferably including the star in question. The next step involved pointing the scope to the right bit of sky using the Telrad, then looking through the optical finder (which I'd long since upgraded to a 9x50 model) to identify the patterns I'd picked out with the binoculars. Sounds simple, right? Well, it got the job done – eventually. In this case I was soon able to focus on 38 Gem, which at 55x was peanut-shaped. Increasing the magnification to 89x cleanly split the components, but it took 144x to really bring the color contrast out for this pair. This is often the case with double stars. The primary star was the palest shade of yellow, with the much fainter companion having at most a subtle hint of blue. This is another fairly close pair (seven arc seconds apart) with a significant difference in magnitude: that of the primary is 4.7, with the companion at magnitude 7.5. Whatever magnification I applied, 38 Gem's location near the edge of the winter Milky Way made for a beautiful and star-strewn setting for this pretty pair.

Both finding nu Geminorum (it was naked-eye visible) and then splitting it proved no real trouble at all. In fact, it was split by the finder scope! But with a two arc minute separation, that's not very surprising. Using the Newt, I found 55x more than adequate, not only showing the blue-white primary in fine contrast to its bluish, mote-like companion (fourth vs. eighth magnitude), but bringing into view the pleasing field of stars around them. After two relatively close doubles in a row, this duo almost felt like cheating.

The last double I tracked down in Gemini was 15 Geminorum, a much fainter pair than any I'd gone after so far. Finding it proved easier than I might have expected, using nu and 16 Geminorum as landmarks. (Or should that be skymarks?) In fact, I never needed either finder for this one, and just carefully nudged the Newt in the right direction to bring the desired target into view when I was finished absorbing the sight of nu Gem. A magnification of 55x was good enough to split this pair which, while much fainter than my other targets thus far (seventh magnitude primary and a ninth magnitude companion), displayed very clear yellow and blue color contrast. At 89x the colors were amazingly clear. Something about the relatively dim magnitudes, combined with the clear color contrast between the components, made them feel incredibly remote compared with the stars I'd been observing up to then. It seemed I was looking deeper in the galaxy, or into another realm altogether.

By this point in the night, Gemini had settled so far toward the western horizon that the low angle was working against the otherwise good seeing conditions. So I left the Twins to their travels, wondering if I'd have a chance to work in that constellation again before these boys were lost in the sun for the season. If not, at least I can rely on their return next year. Sometimes I think the constancy of the stars is a large part of what draws us out into the gentle night with our telescopes. It's good to have something you can count on to such a high degree.

Iota Cancri is another double star that I've observed before, with a pale yellow and cool blue color contrast comparable to that of 15 Geminorum, but involving a much brighter primary star (fourth magnitude) with a sixth magnitude companion separated by about 30 arc seconds. I had no trouble splitting the pair at 55x, but once again a bit more magnification (89x) served to better bring out the color contrast. Some listings consider this duo a "showpiece." I completely agree.

Having done a couple of open double stars in a row, most of them with significant contrasts in color and magnitude, phi 2 Cancri came as something of a surprise. It took binoculars and both finders to work my way to this pair, which at a combined magnitude of six was well below naked-eye detection from my back yard. When I found what I thought was the right star, a magnification of 55x showed not a hint of this being a double star. It was oblong at 89x and finally split pretty cleanly at 144x, revealing a set of twin diamonds glittering all of 5 arc seconds apart. These stars are a matched set, looking absolutely identical to my eye, whichever eye I put to the eyepiece. And there was a silvery quality to their glitter, as if they were somehow a touch metallic, rather than simply pure white.

Zeta Cancri ended up being the last double for the night, though it was anything but the last one on the list. (I always end up with lists that are a little longer than is truly reasonable.) At 55x this pair was another stellar peanut, barely split at 89x, but definitely separated at 144x. These stars appeared yellow to me, plain and simple yellow, and of matching hues as far as I could tell. There was a difference in magnitude, fifth for the primary star and sixth for its companion; nothing dramatic, but quite noticeable. The guidebook I brought out with me (*A Visual Atlas of Double Stars* by Mike Ropelewski) mentioned a third member, a close companion to the primary star that should be visible to observers with a "sizable instrument." I'm not sure what the author meant by sizable, but apparently the Newt doesn't qualify. I pushed the magnification to 230x, but though I thought I could just barely see some elongation in the primary star, it remained a single star. Someday, on a night of truly superb seeing, I'll "Barlow" one eyepiece or another and see what happens.

If you haven't felt the allure of double-star observing, you might find it odd that eight such targets could eat up an evening's worth of eyepiece time. It's just stars, after all, two by two. And yet as I came to zeta Cancri I found myself running short on time. It all takes time, of course, especially the part about hunting the sky for a specific target. Since I actually enjoy the challenge involved in doing so, I count that time well spent. But there's something else, something harder to put into words. With double stars, as with any other aspect of visual observing, a timeless quality to the experience takes hold and I can't feel the minutes ticking by. I find this to be true even though I record the time of each observation I make. It's as if the times I record are not measures of time's passage, but static and arbitrary markers of some sort. I can note a specific time on the log sheet, but when I'm at the eyepiece I can't really feel that time has passed, and so I am usually brought up short at some point by how late it's gotten to be, no matter how many objects I manage to observe. Each double star (or nebula, or galaxy, or crater) the Newt sends through an eyepiece and into my mind becomes an experience that steps slightly outside of time, and I don't really know how long I sit there gazing through that little bit of glass. The time passes, and yet the experience is timeless.

DARK SKIES IN THE WEST

The dark-sky site I use most often has the distinction of being the only astronomy site I've heard of that includes an aircraft runway. It's miniature, built for various model aircraft, but still – it's a runway. You can see it in Google Earth images.

The Tucson Amateur Astronomy Association maintains an observing site about forty minutes west of my part of town. Known by the acronym TIMPA (Tucson International Modelplex Park Association), the site is readily accessible and popular, especially with new amateur astronomers. There's a substantial light dome to the east, often referred to as the "Tucson Nebula," and some light pollution very low in the north from Marana and Casa Grande. The skies overhead and to the west and south are very good. Best of all, the site is dominated by desert scrub; there are no tall trees, just a scattering of mesquites that don't block the horizon unless you practically set up under one.

There have been afternoons when I've set up the Newt near sunset while model aircraft hobbyists are still doing their thing. I've seen many sorts of aircraft, in scale-model form, take off and then eventually return to that miniature airstrip. There's even been a miniature helicopter. A local model rocketry group uses the site as well, and now and then a night launch event takes place on a scheduled observing night. The rockets are certainly a noisy distraction, and the LEDs attached to them aren't always night-vision friendly, but it's cool nonetheless to see them fly.

Normally, though, a TIMPA night is just about stargazing.

On one such occasion I drove out to TIMPA directly into a uncomfortably bright sunset, through a hot, dry desert anxiously awaiting rain. Times like this, the desert feels as if it's holding its breath in anticipation. Skies clear enough to gladden the hearts of astronomers, in mid-July, are not a welcome sight to other desert dwellers. The tardiness of the summer rains offered opportunities to observe summer celestial treasures at a reasonable hour. Unfortunately, there are other, far less desirable consequences as well.

There was a hot, fitful late afternoon breeze cutting across the site as I set up. We make the usual jokes about it being a "dry heat," but the low humidity does make a difference. Just need to be sure you've brought plenty of drinking water, or that dry heat will wear you down through dehydration. Fortunately the breeze was not stiff enough to kick up a lot of dust, desert dust being harmful to optics. Even at sunset, as I collimated the Newt, the temperatures were just below triple digits (Fahrenheit scale — dry heat, my ass!) Unpleasant as the simmering sunset might have been, still we gathered, knowing how quickly the temperatures would drop with the sun below the horizon. Oh, it would stay very warm, but comfortably so. My own set-up completed, I walked around in the warm dusk, trading greetings with people I knew, and introducing myself to those new to me.

As Twilight faded, the three-day-old Moon glowed low in the west. Venus was a beacon nearby, and Mercury could be picked out in the murky horizon. As I strolled back to my site, lesser nighthawks cut through the air on stiff wings. Bats fluttered past me, often just a few feet over my head.

A look to the southeast revealed one of those less desirable consequences of the dry weather – a ruddy orange glow rising from the far-off Santa Rita Mountains. Wildfires were burning there, and had been for several days, fanned by hot, dry winds. The unsettling glow grew and faded, then flared to a pair of gleaming red beacons. I was not alone noticing the fire burning through the brush and woodlands of those mountains, and more than a few telescopes were turned toward it. Few of us watched the fire for very long; it was too depressing, and for me at least, generated some feelings of guilt, being out there taking advantage of the same conditions that aided and abetted those flames. Foolish, perhaps, but feelings that were unavoidable – for me, at any rate.

Turning from that unpleasant sight, I paid my respects to La Luna, a glorious silver crescent in a dark blue sky, and took some good long looks at Jupiter, Mercury, and Venus. I was out there to pursue more distant targets, but the sky that time of year remains bright in the west for a while after sunset. It was the middle of summer, and true night, in astronomical terms, doesn't come on until after 9pm MST. A late start on DSO observing was unavoidable.

The Moon and bright planets are very easily observed from my back yard, trees notwithstanding. The summertime treasure trove of DSOs is another matter, and so I was understandably eager to get on to the main event. The evening passed and the Moon slipped into the dust-hazed air of the western horizon. The sky darkened and the Milky Way was high in the east. Those who had made the hot drive settled in at eyepieces and behind red-tinted computer screens, and the observing began in earnest.

Ursa Major was on its way out for the season, already low in the northwest by the time it was dark enough for my purposes, so targets in the Great Bear were an immediate priority. I first went after the Messier objects low and outside the bowl of the Dipper. M108 was easily located, but because the sky wasn't quite dark in the west (and the Moon was a nice bright crescent), it was not terribly interesting. I gave it a good, long look all the same, and attempted a sketch. At 230x it was a faint, flattened oblong of grey haze, with what looked like a foreground star almost in the middle. Such a ghostly presence to represent billions of suns; a non-observer would be unimpressed. Knowing what I was looking at made a difference. Something of the same feeling came to me when I examined the Owl Nebula (M97), a spectral grey, subtly mottled globe (at both 144x and 230x, both with an Orion Ultrablock filter), the sort of thing that would make a non-astronomer wonder why we make such a fuss about staying up all night. But this specter in the sky, just barely owl-like with a bit of averted imagination, marks the grave of a star. I sketched what I saw, and tried to show appropriate respect.

From home, the southern summer sky might as well not exist, even when evening thunderstorms are not blowing themselves out over Tucson. Looking south from my back yard, I peer over a rooftop that's been baking in the sun all day. The heat rising from the roof makes observing in that direction problematic at best. So the objects in that region had a high priority, and as soon as my two targets in Ursa Major were taken care of, the Newt was aimed in a southerly direction. Faced with the embarrassment of riches present in the vicinity of Scorpio and Sagittarius, the problem quickly became one of deciding what to observe with only a single night at my disposal. I started out with an easy decision and put the Newt on M4, a beautiful star cluster, and classified as a globular cluster. It looked to me (89x) as if someone accidentally turned the cluster's gravity off, leaving the cluster to spread out and lose definition. There was little if any concentration near what should have been the core, and it was ragged around the edges. Don't get me wrong, this is a beautiful star cluster, crossed by complicated patterns made by ropes and strings of stars. But if I hadn't read up on it using reliable sources, I might not have guessed it was a globular cluster at all.

For a nearby contrast in defining globular clusters, there's M80 – a Messier designation that conjures noisy memories of Fourth of July celebrations long past. Now *this* is a globular cluster, round and well defined with a distinctly visible core region when examined at 89x. The distinction between core and halo was clearer at 144x. Although the seeing was only average (to use the Clear Sky Chart's assessment for that night), M80 responded well to extra magnification, and at 230x the cluster developed a dusty look, with many stars on the edge of resolution.

A fellow club member was set up next door with

a ten-inch reflector on a Dobsonian mount. Hearing sounds of amazement from him, I asked what he had in the eyepiece, and the answer was, "Triffid Nebula." It was on my list anyway, so I tracked that one down next, having had only poor views of it in town to that point. When I had M20 in view, I found myself in full agreement with my neighbor. At 89x it was pretty impressive, and with or without the Ultrablock filter, it took magnification well. I found my best views at 89x with a filter, and 144x without, with each view having something to offer. Dark lanes separated ghostly patches of light, and all of it was decorated by an open scattering of stars. In the end, I found myself preferring the filtered view. Without the narrow-band filter, the Triffid was a close double star with a grey patch around it. The nebulosity was obvious, but not striking. With the filter the nebula was the complex structure you would expect to see, with brighter lobes of interstellar clouds divided by dark lanes that seemed to more or less converge on the double star. I spent some time with the Triffid, long enough to make a satisfactory sketch.

When I was done, and since I was in the area, I switched to the Lagoon Nebula, M8. It was the subject of my first experiment with a narrow-band filter, done from the back yard, where I could detect the Lagoon Nebula, but not make much of it. Adding the filter brought it out to a surprising degree and made me very happy I'd purchased that Orion Ultrablock filter. I wondered what difference would be made by using the filter under darker skies. Such an intriguing sight, at home, that patchy cloud of glowing dust with a sparkling cluster on one edge. To see as much of it as possible at one time, I used as low a magnification as I could manage that night. Instead of increased magnification I added the Ultrablock filter. Quite a difference, indeed! The open star cluster associated with the nebula was no longer a near neighbor, but actually within the nebulosity. That was something I missed in town, even with the filter. The scene was so amazing it was easy to ignore the slight color shift of the stars in the cluster (a bit blue to my eyes) caused by the filter. The cloud of nebulosity was not uniform, and was marked by darker patches, with something of a dark lane running east to west not far from the cluster.

The Lagoon held my attention for quite some time, and caught the fancy of my neighbor, who borrowed the filter and soon committed himself to making such a purchase in the near future.

The Butterfly Cluster (M6) was easily seen by eye alone, and was spectacular in binoculars. In a low-power eyepiece with a generous field of view, it's a true showpiece object. Looking this low in the southern sky did affect the seeing conditions, which otherwise ranged from average to good over the course of the night. Alternately warm and relatively cool breezes ruffled atlases and observing logs as the steadily dropping temperatures induced instability, stirring up the air. The Butterfly Cluster sometimes flickered and danced, depending on the temperature of the breeze.

By the way, no matter how much averted imagination I apply, I just can't see a butterfly when I study M6.

M7, sometimes known as the Ptolemy Cluster, was even lower in the sky, and a bit difficult to observe well when the breezes came and went. M7 is a bright, loose cluster of stars, sort of a southern Pleiades. With a bit of patience, I obtained the sketch I desired. I was working on the Messier Catalog that night, and for Astronomical League purposes, the sketch was essential.

Saturday night was behind and Sunday morning was in progress. Only my neighbor remained of the earlier crowd. Considering how late in the evening it had been before it was dark enough to do serious observing, I was baffled that people were so quick to call it a night. I was getting tired, but not to the point that I'd be in danger on the drive home. I have an agreement with my wife about safety issues involved with trips to dark-sky sites. I don't stay out late enough to be a hazard driving, and I don't stay in an isolated location as a solo act. It turned out my neighbor was working under similar rules, and we kept tabs on each other. A fine balance, between keeping each other honest and not wanting to be the one who pulled the plug.

Wandering through Sagittarius, actually on my way to a specific object, I came upon a globular cluster. Imagine what it must have been like to be Messier, slowly scanning the heavens and coming across such sparkling enigmas. Another 'nebula without a star' would have been his impression. But I know what I'm looking at, so in place of an enigma I see a beautiful globular cluster. In this case the globular in question turned out to be M22. At 89x it looked somewhat irregular in its outline, with a bit of a glittery look to it, like stars embedded in smoke. At 144x there seemed to be many stars just on the edge of resolution, and the M22 had a grainy look to it.

Conversation with my observing partner of that night, regarding M31's companion galaxies, prompted me to look at M31. Andromeda was well up in the east, and far enough away from the light dome of Tucson that I could make out the galaxy with my eyes alone. At 55x I could just get M31, M32, and M110 in the same field of view – but just barely. It was quite a sight, squeezed in as it was. The same conversation reminded me of another feature of Andromeda, and I talked him into swinging that Dobsonian down to Mirach. The Ghost of Mirach was easily visible that night, in both an eight-inch and a ten-inch scope.

By this point it was pushing 3 am and, like it or not, I was encroaching the limits of my endurance. I made noises about packing it in, my neighbor agreed, and we examined the Double Cluster. On a lark (the seeing had steadied and was very good) I pushed magnitude for all it was worth trying to see the central star in the Ring Nebula (M57). Knowing my chances were slim to none, I was neither surprised nor disappointed that it wasn't visible. Still, with the narrowband filter and 144x I had one of the best looks at the Ring ever. After a pause to increase my blood sugar and caffeine levels a bit (in anticipation of the drive home) I revisited M11, taking a good look at this cluster under dark skies for the first time. It was richer and brighter than I expected from the view at home, a fine sight with which to end the evening.

Still reluctant to do so, my friend and I packed up and drove out; I pulled the gate closed behind us and we went our separate ways. To that point in my observing career it was the best and most productive night under dark skies I'd experienced. I blessed the delayed Desert Monsoon, then saw the pulsing glow of the Santa Rita fire. It was a sobering moment. The drought-stricken desert was lost in the darkness beyond the headlamp beams. Now and then I caught a glimpse of a coyote or a desert cottontail rabbit. It seemed much darker, now that I was reliant on two beams of bright white light; contrast will do that, especially when you're as tired as I was by then.

And I was, indeed, tired. I was at my limit, and while it's useful to know where the lines are drawn, I really should have left a slightly wider margin for error. Luckily the city streets, when I returned to town, were all but deserted; I made it home without incident. At home, I left everything locked in the car and went to bed. A few hours later I roused myself and talked my wife into going out for breakfast, and I regaled her with tales of my observations. Running our usual Sunday errands, I was surprised by how well food and coffee had revived me. Just before lunch, I stretched out on the bed for a moment. The next thing I knew it was 5 pm.

I have this strange memory of my wife folding the laundry on me. But I may have imagined that.

A FINE AND QUIET LUNACY

I've always been in love with the Moon. As a child I was fascinated by its phases and the mottling that made it look vaguely like a benign face peering down from the sky. As a boy I became completely caught up in the space race, with its lunar objectives. I spent more time during my youthful astronomy phase looking at the Moon than anything else in the night sky. And when the Three-legged Newt became my instrument of choice so many years later, I went back to Moon-watching without giving it a second thought.

For my backyard observing location, the best times for lunar observing come between late winter and the beginning of summer. The weather is usually clearest and most comfortable in April and May, so many of my lunar notes have dates in those two months. I've observed the Moon no few times, and if I extracted all the lunar observations I've made with the Newt from the logbook and placed them in chronological order, it would make a book of considerable length. I'll be merciful, however, and offer only a modest sample.

An April Moon

It was a calm, quiet, and fairly cool night for Moon-watching, with clear skies and seeing conditions that were above average, as the Clear Sky Chart rates such things. I put on a sweatshirt and set up the Newt under a seven-day-old Moon.

I started out with Cassini and its internal craterlets A and B. Calling these craters (especially A) crater-*lets* seems a bit misleading to me. Unlike their namesakes in Plato, at 89x you don't squint through the eyepiece hoping to catch a glimpse of Cassini A and B. You can hardly miss these two pockmarks, especially when they contain that yin-yang combination of shadow and blazing light that craters often sport in the lunar morning. (The terminator wasn't all that far to the west, relative to Cassini.) They dominated the interior of the otherwise smooth main crater. Cassini is flooded with now frozen lava, hence the smooth floor. The rising magma seems to have altered the outer rim of the crater, leaving the apron of debris surrounding Cassini looking partially melted. Cassini A and B mar the smooth floor of the main crater, with Cassini A not quite round. Between Cassini A and the main crater rim the ground looked rumpled. Just there; everywhere else the interior of the crater looks smooth.

The area just outside the rim of Cassini (which itself seems to barely rise above the surrounding mare) is as interesting as the crater itself. There is an incomplete collar of rougher terrain around Cassini that hugs the rim, but does not extend very far from it, east and north. This material looks like it was softened by the heat of the lava around it, and slumped like half-melted snowdrifts. It's relatively broad and uniform, and paler than the

Moonscape surrounding it. As you come around the west side, to the vicinity of Cassini M (a craterlet more deserving of that term on the outside of the rim) the collar pulls up closer to the crater rim and looks less melted, and more intact. Near the lowest point of the rim (south side) the collar is all but invisible. The appearance it presents is that a ring – the crater itself – was set into the still molten mare surface, and that material melted and spread slightly away from the ring before things cooled.

Although they were not part of the observing plan, I couldn't help taking a look at the Montes Alpes nearby. The various peaks and prominences in that blocky landscape cast fantastical shadows that gave the area the look of a lunar Himalaya. The Moon is covered with distractions of this sort. All of my lunar observing plans are interrupted this way on a regular basis.

Sinus Lunicus is on the list of targets for the Astronomical League's Lunar II observing project. I assume this is because it is the site of the first physical contact between human beings and the Moon. As lunar features go, it doesn't have much besides history to recommend it. The contact was the impact of the Soviet Lunik 2 probe, which may not seem like much of a distinction, but every adventure has to start somewhere and somehow. I never used more than 144x here. Sinus Lunicus proper offers little for the lunar sightseer, but the surrounding neighborhood is a fine place to explore with a good atlas. Archimedes, Aristillus, and Autolycus together made a fine spectacle, with the sunlit heights of the Montes Spitzbergen blazing silver against the dark side of the terminator; the rest of the range was lost in shadows. Around Aristillus the "un-melted" version of the debris collar visible around Cassini was plain to see. Sinus

Lunicus appeared to be bounded, east and west, by low dorsae I could not find labeled on the maps I brought out.

Linne was a sort of borderline target, at this point in a lunation; there's no shadow relief to speak of and the tiny crater is almost completely full of sunshine. It was an interesting feature to contemplate, all the same. At 89x it was a round, white spot out in the western third of Mare Serenitatis. To look at it under that lighting, with that magnification, it's hard to believe that this is a crater at all. Even at 230x the true nature of the marking was sometimes invisible when the air was less than steady. I don't find it at all difficult to believe that some observers thought this crater had, at one time, disappeared.

The Moon is a bit cracked, a trait it shares with a few amateur astronomers. One set of these cracks, Rima Ariadaeus, wasn't in the best lighting possible, but at 144x showed up quite nicely. I could trace it almost all its length, long and straight, from its namesake crater at the east end to well past Silberschlag. Where Rima Ariadaeus passes Silberschlag, a spur or ridge jutting north from that crater seems to cut across the rille. Rukl's atlas shows a branch at each end of the rille, and I could just barely make out something of the sort near the east end. The west end counterpart was lost to me.

Rima Hyginus was another unplanned diversion, but the angle of sunlight and the shadow relief it created was such that I couldn't pass it up. In any case, I was in the neighborhood. At 144x it opened in a wide, shallow arc toward the gouges and debris that mar so much of the region between it and Mare Imbrium. The middle of the bend in the rille is marked by the crater Hyginus. The northwestern branch held more shadow than the southeastern half. Something about the way it seems to balance on the point marked by crater Hyginus makes this one of the Moon's more dramatic rilles.

But back to the regularly scheduled program, which happened to include more cracks to explore. Lunar observing is a matter of getting the timing right, for many features on the face of the Moon. Observe too early and the desired feature is lost in the shadows at and beyond the terminator. If you wait too long the sun will be so high in the lunar sky – think "high noon" – that no shadows are cast, and for some features the lack of shadow relief can render them invisible. Nowhere is this more evident than in the observation of lunar rilles, which under a high sun can be all but invisible; exaggerated by shadows, they are pretty easy to spot. I zoomed in on Rimae Treisnecker, quite visible this night, and spent some time trying to trace out all its branches. This wasn't my first examination of the region, so with that experience to guide me I did pretty well. I could easily pick out the main course, running north from Rhaeticus to the sharp bend east of Treisnecker, northeast to another shallow bend, and from there northwest until it faded out into the lunar surface. The lesser rilles running north and south from the big bend were easy to see when I nudged the magnification up to 230x, but I was only able to do so briefly as the seeing conditions were deteriorating by then, and showing no sign of settling back into the earlier, better conditions. At lower powers the rilles that were visible all looked thin and spidery, as if delicately etched into the surface of the Moon, an appearance that surely belies the true breadth and depth of these cracks in the Moon.

And then, in late May...

Bullialdus and its associated craters were situated well away from the terminator, but appeared to show a fair amount of detail-revealing shadow relief all the same. The west-facing inner wall of the crater held just a hint of shadow that at 89x seemed oddly diffused, as if a faint light filled it. It was not the well-defined sort of shadow you see bisecting craters earlier in the lunar day when they sit closer to the terminator. It was likely caused by sunlight spilling across the western inner wall at a shallow angle, clipping the tips of terraces or piles of debris, and illuminating them, even though as individual features they were too small to see. In contrast, the inner wall on the east side, in full sun, seemed marked by bright, curved lines which might have been terraces, utterly lacking in shadows.

The crater, at low magnification, puzzled me. It seemed out of kilter, or misaligned. It took a while and a higher magnification (144x) to puzzle out what I was seeing. The confusion was rooted in the broken central peak, which was centered relative to the crater rim, but not relative to the flat part of the crater floor. The flat crater floor looked smaller than I would have expected for the diameter of the rim, and at first glance seemed somehow displaced. The explanation seems to be that the inward slumping of material that followed the impact creating this crater was uneven, sliding more from the west than the east. This would have happened after the impact, which explains the central peak being centered relative to the rim, not the crater interior. This partial coverage of the floor, inside an otherwise normal crater rim, made the entire scene seem distorted. Was what I saw the truth of the matter, or a shadow-shaped illusion? A trick of the light? The Moon has no shortage of those. Perhaps future observations – and research using the references at my desk – will clarify this issue.

The two companion craters to the south that are designated Bullialdus A and B are both of about the same apparent size, but otherwise differ from one another significantly. The wall of Bullialdus A looks lower, and the floor is smoother and darker, than the same features in Bullialdus B. I was not able to be entirely sure (seeing did not support 230x) but there seemed to be a small central peak in Bullialdus B. The mare material around Bullialdus proper looked darker to the west than to the east.

My first look at the Hainzel crater complex (hammered mess would be a better phrase for it) was at 89x. Being quite close to the terminator, the eastern inner wall (or should I say 'walls'?) was obscured by a thick black band of shadow. Hainzel and Hainzel A were well-lit and I could see curved terrace-like structures on the east-facing inner wall of Hainzel A, and a bright spot like a modest central peak. Part of Hainzel proper was hidden by shadow cast by the broken wall of Hainzel C that runs ridge-like up the central southern half of the complex. Of the three, Hainzel A looks most recent, and intact. If I understand anything at all of lunar stratigraphy, Hainzel A really is the relative youngster of the set, with Hainzel C the middle child, and Hainzel itself the first born. Being the oldest of five myself, I can relate to its battered condition!

To the north then, for a look at the peaks of Mons Gruithuisen Gamma and Delta. I used 89x to pick them out, and then as usual increased magnification until the view broke down. Unfortunately, the view broke down very quickly. The seeing rather abruptly degraded to A4, with long moments of A5. When I looked at the Moon with my eyes alone I half expected to see it shimmering in the sky. One more time with 144x, and with a lot of patience, I managed to study these rounded mountains at the edge of Mare Imbrium. Both peaks cast shadows that were in area roughly equal to the mountains themselves. Mons Gruithuisen Gamma, the northernmost of the pair, looked rounded and more symmetrical than Mons Gruithuisen Delta, which has an irregular outline.

Running northeast from Delta toward, and just touching, the outer rim of Mairan A, is a somewhat S-shaped ridge. According to the maps and pictures I've seen of these exaggerated lunar domes, Gamma sports a craterlet near its center, but no matter how long I looked I couldn't pick up on this feature.

Eventually patience was worn down by truly atrocious seeing conditions, and even low-power views were unrewarding. It was time to give it up, which – with great reluctance – is just what I did.

RANDOM ESSAYS

‡

THAT NEWBIE FEELING

I've often said, in print and otherwise, that no matter how many nights I spend under the stars, or out there soaking up Moonlight, there usually comes a moment when I feel like a complete novice. The Three-legged Newt only sharpened that perception by widening the view, so to speak. Oh, the motions I go through getting geared up are familiar enough, and the patterns of stars overhead have long since been committed to memory. And yet every night I'm out there, no matter which telescope I use, the feeling is there, the feeling that I'm just standing on the edge of it all.

I was not at all surprised to feel this way so strongly when I started using the Three-legged Newt. After several months of revisiting boyhood memories with the Old Scope, re-familiarizing myself with the Moon and stars, and of re-acquainting myself with the sort of views 60mm can give you, the increase to eight inches of aperture was a shock to the system. Those first views through the Newt were nothing short of a revelation. In many cases I really *was* seeing things for the first time, given how many deep-sky objects and lunar features the Newt can 'see' that are beyond Old Scope's resolving power. But unlike an amateur astronomer who starts out fresh with a telescope having decent aperture, I already knew my way around the sky pretty well by the time the Newt came into my life. I was so deeply into stargazing as a teenager that my parents grew concerned about the amount of time I spent alone, out in the dark. And although the better part of three decades passed before I took up astronomy again as a serious pursuit, I managed to remember enough of the essentials that the inevitable and necessary refresher course brought me back up to speed fairly soon. And yet the sense of unending novelty survived.

You might expect that lunar observing would be one aspect of visual observing in which experience would soon overcome novelty. But the Moon, in its own cold, grey way, still leaves me feeling like a beginner each time I aim a telescope up at it. I know my way around La Luna pretty well, but no two visits are ever precisely the same. In large part this is because slowly changing degrees of libration and the fact that the combined motions of the Moon and Earth don't line up exactly the same way from one lunation to the next. So the view changes in subtle ways – more or less the same, but not quite. Observe the Moon long enough and you'll see what I mean. Familiar features will inevitably surprise you.

Of course, any celestial object observed for the first time *should* invoke a feeling of newness. That only stands to reason. And so you would expect repetition of certain sights to take the edge of newness off the experience. But simple repetition doesn't seem to change things as much as I might have expected. It doesn't matter how often I put Saturn in the eyepiece, it never comes down to a routine "Okay, there it is" reaction. Quite the contrary, whenever the ringed world is in view and the seeing is good it never fails to startle me with its beauty. Or consider the Orion Nebula. How many times can I look at M42 and still find myself caught somewhat by surprise by the realization that I am looking into a place where stars are born? Well, so far it's happened every single time. Familiarity has never blunted the sense of wonder such a sight invokes in me, and it seems to me that wonder is the thing that prevents the once-novel experience from ever growing routine. Having the larger telescope available has only fed that sense of wonder.

But there's more to that persistent newbie feeling than the increase in aperture. Even if aperture has caused me to see familiar sights in very different ways and a sense of wonder protects me from boredom, over time I've discovered that this feeling is rooted in something deeper. At the heart of the matter is the almost instinctive realization that I know virtually *nothing at all* in the grand astronomical scheme of things, that what I've seen so far is an utterly insignificant fraction of what's out there. This remains true, thirteen years after the Three-legged Newt had its First Light, and was just as true all those years ago with the Old Scope. The feeling of astonishing newness is strongest in the wee hours at a dark-sky site, when I'm tired and no longer quite so focused on the view through the eyepiece. Maybe you've had something like this experience yourself, when the sky is dark and clear, the stars hard and bright, when fatigue frays the boundary between reason and imagination. Your feet seem barely in touch with this Earth and you can almost feel the sky drawing you up and outward. Your mind tries to take it all in and the night sky overwhelms you as if you've never before beheld its infinite depth. It doesn't matter how often I get out there, a moment comes when it catches me like this, and I can barely breathe. It's so much more than mind and imagination can take in that I feel as though I am starting all over again. I feel as if I *must*...

It makes perfect sense to feel this way, when you think about it. That's a big universe out there. No matter how much of it I manage to see in my lifetime, I will always be just getting started.

TERMINATOR SLIDE

I prefer to follow a plan when I get the chance to spend time at the eyepiece. Following a process step by step toward a specific goal comes naturally to me, so a planned observing session (and the planning process itself) is part of what I enjoy when I indulge in amateur astronomy. I know some amateur astronomers who shake their heads when they hear me say such a thing, finding my approach too restrictive. "Too much like work," they say. But as my long-gone grandmother was fond of saying, "You can't call it work if you enjoy it," which I do. There are, however, occasions when carefully planning an observing session just isn't an option. Perhaps the weather changed in a way the forecasters didn't expect, providing clear skies when I didn't count on them. Or maybe a prior commitment comes to nothing. Whatever the reason, I sometimes find myself with a clear evening, unexpectedly free and, well, clear. If it truly comes at the last moment, there might not be enough time to draw up the sort of plan I prefer. But you can bet your aperture that I don't waste the opportunity, *especially* when the Moon is available.

If there is a perfect object for an impromptu observing session, it's surely the Moon. With absolutely no advanced planning I can spend hours exploring its surface, simply playing tourist and taking in the sights. I cannot imagine ever growing bored with the face of the Moon. Every visit reveals something new, or gives me a changed perspective on otherwise familiar scenery. And although I have no real travel plan, I don't simply poke around at random. I go to the north end of the lunar terminator, that stark and unearthly division between day and night that defines the phases of the Moon, and follow its shallow sliding curve across the face of the Moon from the north pole to the south. I pause along the way whenever something catches my eye and fancy, and believe me when I say that I make a lot of stops. The terminator is where it's at, the scenic route most often traveled by watchers of the Moon. This is where the shadows of night and the new light of day show off the lunar landscape at its most dramatic. Some shadows are smooth curls of night cast on the floors of shallow craters; others exaggerate the ruggedness of the rims and peaks that cast them. Shadow relief makes it plain to see features and details that would be all but invisible otherwise, and will soon be very hard to pick out of the Moon's grey surface as the lunar "day" progresses from one earthly night to the next. Craters along the terminator may be filled with darkness, with their upper rims shining in stark contrast. Mountains beyond the terminator, out where the night still holds, catch the first rays of the sun with their uppermost peaks and blaze like beacons of white fire. In the highlands it all becomes a maze of curved rims and jumbled terrain, a patchwork of midnight and daylight that weaves back and forth across the dividing line. Where the terminator crosses the plains of the maria, it's a somewhat different story, though surely a variation on a theme in grey rock, jet black shadow, and unadulterated sunshine. Small craters become bottomless black pits in the bleak surface of the plain, and the smallest irregularity in that seemingly smooth mare surface casts long, bold shadows that point to where night remains. Subtle ripples in the ancient frozen stone are clearly etched by shadows clinging to their western sides, and in some cases the shadow is made bolder by the contrasting brightness of sun-facing slopes and exposures. Anything with depth is filled with ink; anything that rises above the surrounding surface shines on one side and casts a shadow on the other.

And so it goes from pole to pole, features revealed in starkly beautiful detail. With a map or an atlas I can pick out the named features, names we have presumed to attach to rock and rille as if we own the place. And it *becomes* a place with the application of those names, losing some of the jumbled chaos of shadow and light. The names given to features of the lunar landscape, to craters and mountains and rilles, almost make the Moon a human place, an extension of our own world, from which I look up through the eyepiece of a telescope. A place virtually changeless that certainly *seems* to change, at least to the human eye. Take a good look at any given hour, slide down the terminator and get a grip on where it clings to the lunar landscape, then come back in a few hours and slide again. The scenic route will run a slightly different course, with the scenery subtly changed by shortening shadows and the spill of daylight between peaks and through clefts in crater walls. Come back the next night and entirely new landscapes will be revealed, and places you thought you knew the night before will be transformed. A familiar world seen in new ways by an ever-changing play between shadows and light.

DIVIDE AND CONQUER

Acquisition of the Newt wasn't simply the realization of a boyhood dream. An eight-inch Newtonian reflector exceeded anything I'd *ever* hoped to get my hands on when I was younger. I remember First Light vividly: Jupiter, the Moon, and M13. That globular cluster in a 25mm Plössl held my attention so firmly that my feet and knees began to ache due to the length of time I remained at the eyepiece. That spring and the following summer – on those evenings when the summer rains permitted – there were many backyard Tucson observing sessions, and that this was a most satisfactory arrangement is something easily measured by the number of pages in my observing log from that time.

In October 2004 my relationship with the back yard changed. One weekend I drove out to a place called Farnsworth Ranch to join in my first ever dark-sky star party. As such events go, it wasn't perfect, with clouds and wind spoiling things for the most part. But before the weather shut me down I had a chance to use the Newt under dark skies, the first time I'd done any observing under dark skies at all since leaving Illinois many years before. It was a real eye-opener, and with each trip to a dark-sky site, the eyes opened wider. It made it clear what even the moderate light pollution of Tucson concealed, regardless of the aperture now at my disposal.

Up until that time, I'd been enjoying those observing sessions in the back yard. It was all too easy, after that first excursion, to look up and see how paltry the suburban sky really was. It truly could not compare.

This might have led to disappointment and a reduction in evenings spent at the eyepiece, and I know that for some amateur astronomers the dark-sky trap can be a real deal killer. If they can't get out on a moonless night under dark skies, it doesn't count as eyepiece time. Luckily, I'm no faint fuzzy fanatic. Oh, I enjoy hopping galaxies and cruising supernova remnants, but my observing roots are the Moon and double stars, and those roots go deep into nights long past. And not all deep-sky objects are rendered invisible by a suburban sky. Instead of giving up on observing from home, I sorted what I wanted to see according to what might be seen best from a given location.

For some aspects of the night sky, this process is a no-brainer. There's no advantage to observing the Moon from a dark-sky site, far removed from city lights. The Moon is best studied from the comfort of home. There's no need to worry about being truly dark-adapted; you won't be while in town anyway, and the Moon itself will finish off any night vision you have. Leave the lights on. Read that lunar atlas with an ordinary flashlight or the light on the back porch. In fact, I find lunar observing more comfortable if I use white light sources to look at charts and references. The brightness of the Moon, in contrast with the dark of night, can create eyestrain. Having a fairly well-lit environment while Moon-watching can relax your eyes, a clear advantage.

While I don't want to be quite as casual about bright lights in the observing environment when naked eye visible planets are my targets, dark adaptation isn't absolutely vital. Like the Moon, you might as well relax and be comfortable, and observe the planets from home. The single exception to the observe-from-home rule for planets might be Mercury. Where I live, and this is true many places, Mercury hugs the horizon just about at rooftop level. To be honest, I've never found Mercury to be a rewarding telescopic sight in any case, and I'm generally satisfied detecting it by eyes alone in the twilight. For the rest, the back porch is a fine place from which to examine the rings of Saturn, the (formerly) Great Red Spot on Jupiter, the polar caps on Mars, and the phases of Venus. I've even observed Uranus and Neptune from there.

Double stars – if I can find them, I can observe them. At first, I found myself limited to those brighter than fourth magnitude, since they are visible to the naked eye in my back yard. In time, as my star-hopping abilities improved, I worked out methods that brought fainter stars into view. The Newt is equipped with two finder scopes: a 9x50 optical finder, and a Telrad. I also keep a small pair of binoculars handy. Using star charts, I learned to determine where a target should be relative to the stars I *can* see. I can then examine that area with the binoculars, and identify fainter stars that are depicted on the charts. I look for patterns in those stars, then use the Telrad to aim the Newt at the right area. Through the 9x50 finder I relocate the same star patterns; I'm generally successful at this, and can steer the Newt to what I want to see. It works the first time more often than not, though there are times when patience and persistence are certainly required.

Open star clusters begin to mark out a sort of transition zone, or grey area, for me. Many of these look pretty good in the Newt from my back yard, but the results definitely vary from one cluster to another. The brighter, more scattered open clusters perform best. Denser gatherings of fainter stars are often reduced to hazy patches of light when viewed from home. When I encounter an example of this, I make a note that this is a cluster worthy of inclusion on a dark-sky expedition list. Even if I suspect this might be the case, I'll still give the star cluster a try. Knowing how to find an object before I head out of town means I'll locate it sooner under those darker skies, and time saved during an all-too-rare dark-sky excursion is precious.

Globular star clusters fit squarely into that grey area between only at home and only under dark skies. There are a lot of globular clusters up there that I can locate and examine from home, but they do lose something. Some of them are almost not worth the bother. When I first observed M13 in Hercules with the Newt, my mind was blown. When I looked at it for the first time under dark skies, it was like seeing something for the first time. It made that kind of difference. And so it is with globular clusters in general; they look so much better under dark skies that I rarely include one in an at-home observing list.

Planetary nebulae share the grey area. A few, when enhanced by an OIII filter, are quite observable from in town. Quite a few, in fact, and even the smaller ones can at least be seen without question. Do they look better under dark skies?

Most do, but for some it really makes no difference; it's the filtered vs. unfiltered view that matters for me. This is a category of deep-sky object that I often hunt down from the back yard, and then add to a dark-sky list for a comparative observation. If the view isn't what I'd hoped for, I note that this is a "try again" for a suitable dark-sky session.

With filters, various bright nebulae can be observed from my back yard, but most are much better – with or without filters – out under dark skies. Here I leave the grey area behind and head into true dark-sky territory. For the most part this class of objects goes on the out-of-town list. (There is a noteworthy exception to this: the Orion Nebula, M42. I don't care where I am, when that one is high in the sky on a clear night, it ends up in the eyepiece sooner or later.) Even further from the heart of the grey area are supernovae remnants. I can find the Crab Nebula in Taurus, but really seeing anything worth reporting requires a trip to a dark-sky site. The Veil Nebula? I've yet to catch a glimpse of it from home. I know it's possible to do so with the right combination of aperture and conditions, but so far, I haven't managed it.

I've observed galaxies a time or two from home – M31, Mirach's Ghost, the Leo Triplet – but these are very definitely exceptions to prove the rule. Most of the galaxies I've tried to track down were either barely detectable ghostly glows, or were not visible at all. Out under dark skies, I'll hop galaxies with the best of them. At home, I seek brighter fare.

So, when the Moon is up, that's the plan, with maybe a few double stars for good measure. If the Moon is nearing Full, that's all I'll work with, and believe me when I say that I don't ever feel limited to the Moon. Not now, not ever! And when the Moon is not available for study, I'll tackle whichever planets are up, and sample the many double and multiple stars strewn across the sky. And I'll throw in a few open star clusters, while maybe taking in a planetary nebula or two. When the chance comes to get out of town and away from the lights, it's globular clusters, various nebulae, and the galaxies themselves.

Divide and conquer. It works for me, this way. You won't become Emperor of the Known Universe, and how you shuffle categories will depend on a number of factors, but I do believe you will stand a much better chance of enjoying each observing session to the fullest by selecting the right targets for your observing circumstances.

THEY JUST DON'T MAKE 'EM...

When a hobby has as long a history as that of amateur astronomy, there's going to be change along the way. A lot of change. Technology advances, attitudes evolve, and new participants bring different points of view. This pattern amplifies itself, as change feeds a cycle of change, and there's truly no going back. I can't see this as a bad thing. A dynamic field of endeavor is attractive to me. I want to see what comes next.

Not everyone looks at it that way.

I've seen how the hobby can change first hand, with the sharpest possible distinction between then and now. There was a long hiatus between my teenage obsession and my return as an adult. When I came back, it seemed almost everything had changed. Ready-to-use telescopes of any quality were only available at prices that stretched somewhat the concept of "affordability." To obtain a good instrument at a reasonable price it was necessary to build it for yourself, and if you were not so inclined then you either contented yourself with a lesser instrument (as I did, though I didn't really know I'd done so at the time – and still don't believe it) or you soon lost interest in astronomy and took up some other hobby. When I drifted away from amateur astronomy after about six years of solitary involvement – if there were others in my home town, I never found them – computers were still mostly science fiction, and not even the sci-fi writers had dreamed up the internet. Celestron had just begun to advertise the SCT, and John Dobson's take on the Newtonian reflector was still a gleam in his eye – if that.

Fast forward to 2003, the year Mars passed so near to the Earth, an event that finally nudged me back into the stargazing habit. By then I was computer-literate enough to think immediately of the internet as a source for information. I was also old-fashioned enough to seek out a local newsstand and buy the current copies of S&T and Astronomy magazines. Imagine my surprise when I started flipping through the pages and saw the bewildering array of astronomy gear – especially the stuff for imaging – being advertised! The situation was immediately compounded when I started typing various search ideas into Google. For me, the change in amateur astronomy from what it was in the 1970s to what it had become in 2003 was a concrete example of future shock. It was the sort of shock you get by jumping into a cold lake on a hot summer day – invigorating!

Those who lived through the changes don't always share that opinion, and I was not in the thick of things for very long before I saw evidence of this discontent. I first became aware of disaffection with modern amateur astronomy as I considered the pros and cons of computer-guided telescopes. The so-called "GoTo" telescope is surely one of those technical innovations that helped to bring a wider variety of personality types into amateur astronomy, by giving the illusion (at least) that object location could be made as simple as pushing a few buttons. The love of convenience has always been a driving force behind innovation. In reading numerous reviews, I kept coming across statements to the effect that the use of a computerized telescope stunted the development of amateur astronomers by somehow preventing them from learning the night sky. But I already knew some people in the local astronomy club who had used nothing *but* GoTo systems, and yet were going out to public star parties explaining the locations of constellations and the motions of planets. While it's easy to imagine someone becoming so dependent on such a technological crutch that the night sky as seen by the naked eye remains a source of confusion, I wasn't seeing this happen.

Seeing no evidence to support such a conclusion, when I eventually decided against buying a computer-guided telescope system, the notion that it might stunt my growth never entered into the equation.

I also, on a regular basis, encountered the opinions of those who treat the dearth of amateur telescope-making in modern times as a sign of the pending end of civilization. Now, it isn't as if *nobody* in amateur astronomy goes into do-it-yourself mode. Nothing could be further from the truth. But it is almost certainly true that a smaller percentage of current amateur astronomers build telescopes than was the case in former days. I have no doubt that there are people today who might have been of a mind to grind a mirror, had they picked up this hobby thirty or forty years ago, who have instead taken advantage of ready-made, high-quality telescopes. But so what? If your goal is to have an instrument with which to explore the universe from your own back yard, and a commercial telescope allows you to cut to the chase, are you a lesser being for taking advantage? Unless you're interested in the building of things for their own sake (certainly a worthy goal) or have a fascination with optics, why would you go to the trouble unless there was some need to do so? That's where I found myself when I came back to this. I want to observe objects in the night sky. For me, the gear is a means to an end, and not the end itself. I have no interest in grinding a mirror, and collimation and star testing is enough optical science for my tastes. There are those who think that makes me an inferior breed of amateur astronomer. I remain untroubled by this, and the thought of building my own telescope was not an option that even remotely crossed my mind while I was deciding which telescope to buy.

Where this 'good old days' philosophy *really* becomes heated is in the realm of astronomy magazines. Both S&T and Astronomy have received some harsh criticism over the years from a small but vocal minority in the world of amateur astronomy. This critique very rapidly extends to any publication that covers anything at all about science for a general audience. The old guard harks back to what they see as the glory days of fatter magazines with fewer advertisements, then looks down its collective nose and sneers at what is being published today because the writers and editors have the temerity to describe the wonders of science (and astronomy in particular) in terms (and with pictures!) that anyone who can read will understand. That the publications have been made more colorful and visually appealing is dismissed as mere sensationalism. This point of view completely ignores the fact that the audience for this sort of material has itself changed significantly over the decades. That audience is broader, with diverse interests and education levels, and has come of age at a time in which the way we relate to information – any and all kinds of information – has been utterly and forever changed from the standards of three or more decades ago. The magazines we read have tracked this change in a simple effort to survive changing times. Whether or not they succeed in the long run remains to be seen, but they will surely not survive by catering to the tastes of an audience that is, quite literally, dying of old age. (I'm serious. I was once told by a former editor of S&T that an all-too-frequent response to a renewal notice was that the subscriber was deceased.) Expecting any publication that has for its subject a rapidly advancing science to remain rooted in the past, in past methods of coverage, is, to put it politely, more than a little unrealistic.

And that is just as true for amateur astronomy as a whole. Yes, it has certainly changed profoundly, and as with all sweeping changes it is possible some good things have been left behind. Change always includes this risk, and an effort should always be made to prevent such losses, to make sure some of the "old school" survives. But at the same time, it only makes sense to embrace the changes that represent the dynamic aspect of a hobby that is based on science and technology.

That newcomers might be more interested in observing objects than in finding them does not make them poor examples of amateur astronomers, any more than a preference for a made-to-order telescope means its owner is lazy, or that a magazine that presents the facts as free of jargon as possible is catering to a less intelligent audience. People drawn to imaging over visual observing are every bit as deserving of the label "amateur astronomer" as those who, like me, sit at the eyepiece. The process of change that has made amateur astronomy accessible to people who have grown up in a more technologically sophisticated society is often dubbed "dumbing down." Consider that phrase, "dumbed down," and the insult it implies for those who enjoy reading the current magazines, following a celestial tour programmed into a GoTo telescope, or using a ready-made Newtonian reflector with a webcam in place of an eyepiece. Then ask yourself why any newbie who encounters it would take the "old school" approach seriously when it seems to be the domain of grumpy curmudgeons?

That's a sure way to make sure this hobby does indeed die of old age.

Fortunately the majority of astronomy hobbyists has embraced these changes. For this reason I'm optimistic that amateur astronomy will not fade into irrelevance, the usual fate of those who deny change.

A FULL KIT

It would seem that, for the foreseeable future, I'm done buying astronomy gear.

This somewhat heretical realization came to me as a quiet bit of insight in October 2008, while with friends under a dark sky. We were comparing and discussing eyepieces, and it occurred to me that the description of my eyepiece collection had an air of finality to it. I found myself swapping eyepieces with fellow observers, comparing the views, and thinking to myself that while there were certainly differences to be seen, they were not of such a degree that I felt compelled to create a shopping list. I was quite satisfied with what I'd pulled together. Later that night, when things had quieted down and I was spending some time observing in a relaxed and solitary state, I found myself extending that eyepiece realization to the general concept of astronomy hobby gear. It was then that I realized I had crossed a particular threshold. For my style of observing, I no longer found myself wishing for an item not yet found in my astronomy tool kit. Five years after rejoining the ranks of amateur astronomers, I had what I needed. It was a full kit, and has felt that way ever since.

You don't need to be involved with amateur astronomy for very long to see that this sentiment is a bit unusual, or at least not often expressed. Even a casual examination of websites devoted to this hobby will show that the discussion of the equipment involved with the making of astronomical observations dominates the discussion of the observations themselves by a significant amount. Which only makes sense, I suppose, since you can argue about which type or brand of eyepiece is best in a given telescope, or for observing particular targets, but whoever argues that the Orion Nebula is a beautiful sight? (And when people become fond of a bit or brand of gear, they can certainly become argumentative.) A visitor to a forum or discussion group hosting such debates will surely be puzzled that so many people have so many different items that all seem to do the same jobs. I know I was baffled when I first began my online investigations. It made for a lengthy selection process, from the telescope itself down to the most recent eyepiece, and for a bumpy learning curve. And while some of the bits and bobs do perform at various levels for various tasks, it takes a while for even the most astute beginner to realize how often those folks who say "X" is the best money can buy are really just saying, "This is the one I bought and I like it better than the others." A very different message, to be sure.

If I've done anything right in the process of staging a comeback, it was taking my time to look past these conflicting opinions as I figured out what I needed, and to slowly fill those needs in a way that made sense for my observing style and financial situation. The idea of trying as much gear as soon as possible, then selling what didn't suit me in the long run (at a loss) never appealed – even if this does appear to be a normal hobby activity for many people. The telescope alone took more than eight months, since I really wanted to get it right the first time. The Three-legged Newt came with a pair of Plössls (25mm and 10mm), and on the advice of the forum folk of Cloudy Nights, I included a good 2x Barlow lens in that initial purchase. Left over from the stop-gap upgrade of my old 60mm refractor were a 6mm Plössl and a 17mm Celestron SMA. That gave me enough of a range of magnifications that I didn't feel an urgent need to quickly fill up an eyepiece case. Making do with these eyepieces was easy, given how good a 60 to 203mm aperture increase would make any eyepiece look.

So I took my time learning to use the Newt, discovering along the way the difference between the observer I thought I wanted to be and the one I became. All the while I followed the never-ending online debates about eyepieces and accessories. I set up a pair of simple mental filters: what sorts of things did *everybody* buy and – regarding eyepieces – what were people with telescopes similar to mine using successfully? Before the first year with the Newt was completed I had a handy portable table, an eye patch, red lights, an observing chair (two actually – as described earlier), a rechargeable power supply, a narrowband filter, a padded case for the OTA, a Telrad... well, you get the idea. I'm quite sure my wife thought I'd completely lost all self-control. If she'd ever spent any time on Cloudy Nights she'd have known I was the model of self-restraint!

Regarding eyepieces, the list that developed led first to the conclusion that I would not be building a collection of "high-end" eyepieces with wide fields of view in this lifetime, since I just cannot justify increasing my debt load for a hobby. So I read what others had to say regarding "lesser" brands and learned about coma, edge correction, fields of view, and the various imperfections that creep in with the compromises made in the name of economy. It was almost a year after buying the telescope that I made a trio of eyepiece purchases: a 9.5mm Orion Lanthanum, a 21mm Orion Stratus, and (because I lucked into a great deal) a 4.8mm Nagler. Among other considerations, these were meant to give me a range of types, magnifications, and fields of view to learn from. I added these new bits of glass in with the originals, and in using them built up a clearer sense of what worked for me, and why.

And I bought books. I've always been a bibliophile, and amateur astronomy has a literature all its own. If I lost my self-control in any way at all – well, a glance at the bookcase behind me, where I sit at my desk, tells that story in a graphic way.

I was into the fourth year of my new incarnation as an amateur astronomer when my experiences as an observer added up to the realization that, while tracking made wide fields of view less essential than might be the case with a Dobsonian mounted reflector, the aesthetics of such views appealed enough to be worth paying for – up to a point dictated by disposable income. This led to what likely will be the last spending spree centered around the Three-legged Newt, and started with the opportunity to buy a lightly used Paracorr. With a way to control the dreaded coma on hand, I was able to consider seriously longer focal length eyepieces, especially two-inch types. Shortly after this purchase, the chance to pick up a 40mm Paragon at a good price came my way. The last spree was capped by picking up the rest of the Stratus line of Orion eyepieces, along with a two-inch OIII filter.

It was on the night of first light for the Paragon and the Paracorr that I realized that the time of gear acquisition had pretty much run its course. Whatever I wanted to study through the eyepiece, I had equipment that would facilitate my interests.

This isn't to say I'm forever done spending money on matters astronomical. There will be inevitable attrition, and of course no one can predict the future. You just never know what will show up in the catalogs. But I am done with looking for items to fill specific *unmet* needs, and most of the "new" offerings in catalogs these days are either imaging-oriented (not a burning desire on my part) or variations on themes of eyepieces and refractors that offer nothing for which I feel a need. In the years since the sight of Mars rekindled the desire to look up by way of an eyepiece, I've come to know myself as an observer. I have a pretty good sense for what I want to do, the goals I want to pursue for the foreseeable future. And now I have what I need to reach those goals, the key elements of which are a fair bit of aperture on a mount that tracks, eyepieces that are comfortable to use and give nice views, wide enough for my tastes, good charts, and a comfortable chair. It's a full kit, and the long delayed fulfillment of a boyhood dream.

I looked at the Veil Nebula in that quiet, chilly night at Farnsworth Ranch and, smiling to myself, realized that I could be content with what I have for a long time.

EPILOGUE

HAVING A SLICE OF SKY

I spent a lot of time, years ago, trying to make it as a writer. Freelance journalism provided a modest living for a while, but what I most wanted to do and be known for was fiction. I wrote a lot of it, but in almost a quarter century of on-again-off-again effort, I never got a break. Not long before my fateful encounter with Mars, I finally gave it up. As bad decisions go, it ranks right down there with growing up in the first place. Mercifully, this hiatus – unlike that separating my teenage astronomy obsession from its older and perhaps wiser counterpart – lasted only a few years, a few unpleasant years during which I learned a hard lesson and an inescapable truth about myself. The digital age and eBooks rolled on to the scene, upending the concept of self-publishing. Like a lot of people, possibly too many people, I jumped at the opportunity. I was writing again, and that was the inescapable truth, that writing was what I most needed to do. Because of the option to self-publish in both eBook and print-on-demand forms, this book and *Mr. Olcott's Skies* (to say nothing of five science fiction novels – so far) had the chance to finally see the light of day.

The start of the brief but awkward writing hiatus coincided – and perhaps it was no coincidence – with my return to stargazing and Moon-watching. For a time my involvement in this hobby was a balm of sorts, a new creative outlet. It wasn't enough, in the long run. Even so, when I started writing for self-publication I had no intention of putting astronomy back on the proverbial shelf. While not as central to my well-being as writing, it was damned important.

For all my good intentions, however, I still don't go out stargazing as often as I did in the years before I launched into self-publishing. It's hard to justify spending time on a hobby when there are so many stories trying to claw their way out of my head. But the night sky can be insistent, and that urge, too, can become overwhelming.

By way of example: a clear evening, typical of the desert in springtime. The constellations of winter, Orion most prominent among them, were low in the west and slipping away. Sirius blazed and glittered in the southwest. Gemini was high in the west, and Leo was straight overhead with Jupiter just within reach of his paws. The arrangement of planet and constellation brought to mind a kitten chasing a toy, a strange fate for the King of Planets. Rising in the east were the constellations of spring and early summer. Boötes was almost horizontal, as if not quite ready to rise and shine from a long seasonal sleep. The Big Dipper was high in the northeast, and the North Star was, well, where you always find it. Plenty to choose from, in terms of targets, even with the narrow bit of sky I can see from the backyard these days.

In 2004, when I bought the new telescope and began to re-educate myself in the art and science of visual astronomy, setting up on the back porch was an eminently workable option. I lost some of the north and northwest sky to the mesquites growing in the back yard, but there were only a handful of constellations I couldn't reach. In the years since, the trees have responded to our care by doing what trees do best – growing. Twelve years later, setting up on the back porch leaves me with somewhat limited observing options, a narrow slice of sky rising from the east, and plunging into the west. On the night in question, I was reminded that even a narrow slice of an infinite universe is a busy place.

Not feeling up for observing challenges, I went for familiar double stars and spent a lot of time looking at Venus and Jupiter. It was a cool, quiet evening that started out a bit windy, but settled to mere whispers of a breeze. The atmosphere was fairly steady, so the seeing conditions were good. The twinkling of stars that you sometimes see, famed in song and nursery rhyme, brings no joy to stargazers. If I'd been able to look up that night and honestly recite "twinkle twinkle, little star," I'd have gone back in to work on the next book. That didn't happen, so I gazed the evening away. If you're at all moved by the sight of stars, just being out on a clear night will do it for you. I spent as much time seated and looking up, eyes alone, as I did at the eyepiece, relaxed and unworried for a while by real world events.

The Muse, however, is never silent, and for all that I focused my attention on Castor and Pollux, Mizar and Alcor, and the Moons of Jupiter, the current work in progress was ever present. Bits of dialogue crept into my thoughts. An idea for resolving a plot wrinkle came to mind. Notes for the book appeared among the observing notes regarding the ruddy gold double star in Leo designated Gamma Leonis. The Muse nudged, but it was gently done, for a change, something always there, but otherwise leaving me at peace under that slice of the night sky. A fact of life, if you're a writer. It never really stops. I felt no conflict between writing and stargazing as this went on, and that's likely because amateur astronomy, being such a blend of knowledge and imagination, is itself a creative thing. Objects in the night sky are utterly beyond my grasp, and so I can only look at them with my eyes or a telescope, touching them with my thoughts alone. I consider what I've read about these things, about how long a star in a double system takes to orbit its companion, about the stars being born in that patch of light beneath Orion's belt, and they assume a reality of sorts for all that they are far beyond my physical reach.

Telling a tale is much the same thing. The worlds I've invented are as unreachable, in their way, as the stars. They are built of knowledge and imagination, but they are *real* in my imagination, as real as the Orion nebula, because I have what I need, through a lifetime of reading and living, to make them seem tangible. And so it seems perfectly natural that, as I look up at the stars, I take their measure even as I imagine people living out there and having adventures. Stars and stories go together and always have, and I am hardly the first to be moved to tell tales while seated beneath them.

A MOON-WATCHER'S NIGHT
BEFORE CHRISTMAS

'Twas the night before Christmas, when all through the house
Not a feline was stirring, nor was my spouse;
The telescope was set up and positioned with care,
For the Moon was shining brightly high up in the air;
The cats were nestled all snug in their beds,
While visions of catnip mousies danced in their brainless heads;
I sat by my telescope, perched on a chair,
And had just settled down for a long lunar stare,
When out in the desert there arose such a clatter,
I sprang from the chair to see what was the matter.
Away from the eyepiece I turned in a flash,
Set aside Rukl and made ready to dash.
The Moon rising high in the dark winter sky,
Gave an illusion of daylight to my adjusted eyes,
And what to those dilated pupils should appear,
But a miniature sleigh, and eight tiny reindeer,

With a little old driver, so lively and quick,
I knew in a moment it must be St. Nick.
More rapid than roadrunners his coursers they came,
And he whistled, and shouted, and called them by name;
"Now, Davy! now, Darney! now, Proclus and Vieta!
On, Cauchy! on Cruger! on Darwin and Billy!
To the top of the mesquites! fly over them all!
Now dash away! dash away! dash away all!"
As mesquite pods that before the wild monsoon storms fly,
When they meet with an obstacle and bounce to the sky,
So up to the house-top the coursers they flew,
And landing they skidded over tiles that were still new.
The wind of their passage blew pages and charts,
And rattled the eyepieces, which gave me a start.
As I settled my papers and was turning around,
Down from the roof came St. Nicholas with a bound
He was dressed in fake fur, from his head to his foot,
And he carefully shook his clothes free of ashes and soot;
"I saw where you were aiming," he said like a true geek,
"And couldn't resist pausing to have a quick peek!"
That Nick was a loonie came as a surprise!
Who'd think an astronomer would wear such a disguise!
His eyes darted toward the eyepiece, clearly drawn to that show,
And his beard so white in the Moonlight did

glow;
    He looked just as I'd imagined, so long ago,
    When my telescope was much smaller and yet
suited me so;
    With a wink of my eye and a nod of my head,
    I stepped from the eyepiece and said, "Go right
ahead!"
    He spoke not a word, but went straight to my
scope,
    And stared at the Moon so long kids elsewhere
lost hope,
    Then shaking my hand he said "Thanks for the
view!"
    And handed me an eyepiece that was shiny and
new.
    He sprang to his sleigh, to his team gave a
whistle,
    And away they all flew out of town like a missile.
    But I heard him exclaim, ere he cruised out of
sight,
    "Merry Christmas to all, and to all a clear night!"

ABOUT THE AUTHOR

Thomas Watson is a science fiction writer and amateur astronomer in Tucson AZ who, because he is a writer, doesn't spend nearly enough time at the eyepiece these days. Having a day job doesn't help, either. Although what that has to do with a hobby that mostly happens at night is hard to say. He also loathes writing about himself in the third person, even if it's considered "professional" in some circles. It sounds pretentious, and besides, it feels like walking backwards up a flight of stairs.